T0026686

A monastery sits on the island Mont Saint-Michel off the coast of France.

Visitors to Bayon Temple in Cambodia travel by elephant.

LITTLE KIDS FIRST BIG BOOK OF THE WORLD

ELIZABETH CARNEY

NATIONAL GEOGRAPHIC KIDS

WASHINGTON, D.C.

CONTENTS

INTRODUCTION 6
HOW TO USE THIS BOOK 7
MAP OF THE WORLD 8

CHAPTER ONE
NORTH AMERICA 10
THE COUNTRIES 12
THE LAND 14
THE WEATHER 16
THE PEOPLE 18
THE ANIMALS 20
THE SIGHTS 22
LET'S GO!
SING IN 3 LANGUAGES 24

CHAPTER TWO
SOUTH AMERICA 26
THE COUNTRIES 28
THE LAND 30
THE WEATHER 32
THE PEOPLE 34
THE ANIMALS 36
THE SIGHTS 38
LET'S GO!
MAKE A RAIN FOREST 40

CHAPTER THREE
EUROPE 42
THE COUNTRIES 44
THE LAND 46
THE WEATHER 48
THE PEOPLE 50
THE ANIMALS 52
THE SIGHTS 54
EXPLORER SPOTLIGHT:
CARSTEN PETER 56
LET'S GO!
BE AN ARTIST LIKE
MICHELANGELO 58

CHAPTER FOUR
ASIA 60
THE COUNTRIES 62
THE LAND 64
THE WEATHER 66
THE PEOPLE 68
THE ANIMALS 70
THE SIGHTS 72
LET'S GO!
DESIGN A MOSAIC 74

CHAPTER FIVE
AFRICA 76
THE COUNTRIES 78
THE LAND 80
THE WEATHER 82
THE PEOPLE 84
THE ANIMALS 86
THE SIGHTS 88
EXPLORER SPOTLIGHT: JANE GOODALL 90
LET'S GO! WATCH ANIMALS LIKE A SCIENTIST 92

CHAPTER SIX
AUSTRALIA 94
THE COUNTRIES 96
THE LAND 98
THE WEATHER 100
THE PEOPLE 102
THE ANIMALS 104
THE SIGHTS 106
LET'S GO! LEAP LIKE A KANGAROO 108

CHAPTER SEVEN
ANTARCTICA 110
THE LAND 112
THE WEATHER 114
THE ANIMALS 116
EXPLORER SPOTLIGHT: ROALD AMUNDSEN 118

LET'S GO! TAKE CARE OF A PENGUIN "EGG" 120

PARENT TIPS 122
GLOSSARY 124
INDEX 126
CREDITS 127

The information in this book is provided for informational purposes only. Please note that some of the activities may be considered strenuous. If the reader has a medical problem or health concern, he or she should consult a medical professional before engaging in any activities.

INTRODUCTION

Would you like to learn about the whole world without leaving this very spot? You can with this atlas! An atlas is a book of maps. What is a map anyway? It's a drawing of a place as it looks from above. This book has maps of the world's continents. You'll see the shapes, locations, and features of Earth's seven major landmasses. On pages 8 and 9, you will see examples of maps that show the land and places on Earth. An atlas usually gives you more information than just maps. In this book, you'll find out about each continent's countries, land and weather, people, animals, and major sights.

NATIONAL GEOGRAPHIC'S *LITTLE KIDS FIRST BIG BOOK OF THE WORLD* IS ORGANIZED BY CONTINENT, FEATURING EVERYTHING A YOUNG EXPLORER NEEDS TO LEARN THE LAY OF THE LAND:

COUNTRIES

Discover maps that present the countries of our world and learn which nations are considered the largest and smallest of their continent.

LAND AND WEATHER

Discover a variety of landscapes with land maps that illustrate each continent's peaks and valleys, waterways and grasslands, and learn about the different types of weather and seasons around the globe.

PEOPLE

Learn about the diverse groups of people who live on each continent. Find out where they came from and how they got there.

ANIMALS

Discover some of the most interesting animals that live on each continent and find out where they make their homes, what they eat, and more.

SIGHTS

Uncover the world's most fascinating sights and the history behind their famous existence.

EXPLORER SPOTLIGHTS

Meet some amazing explorers on missions of discovery around the world and see what they have found.

HOW TO USE THIS BOOK

FACT BOXES give a quick look at important information about a continent. How many countries does it have? Which one is the smallest? Which is the biggest? Which city has the most people? You'll find the answers in the fact boxes.

POP-UP FACTS offer tidbits of really cool information. Use these to impress your friends and family with your geo knowledge.

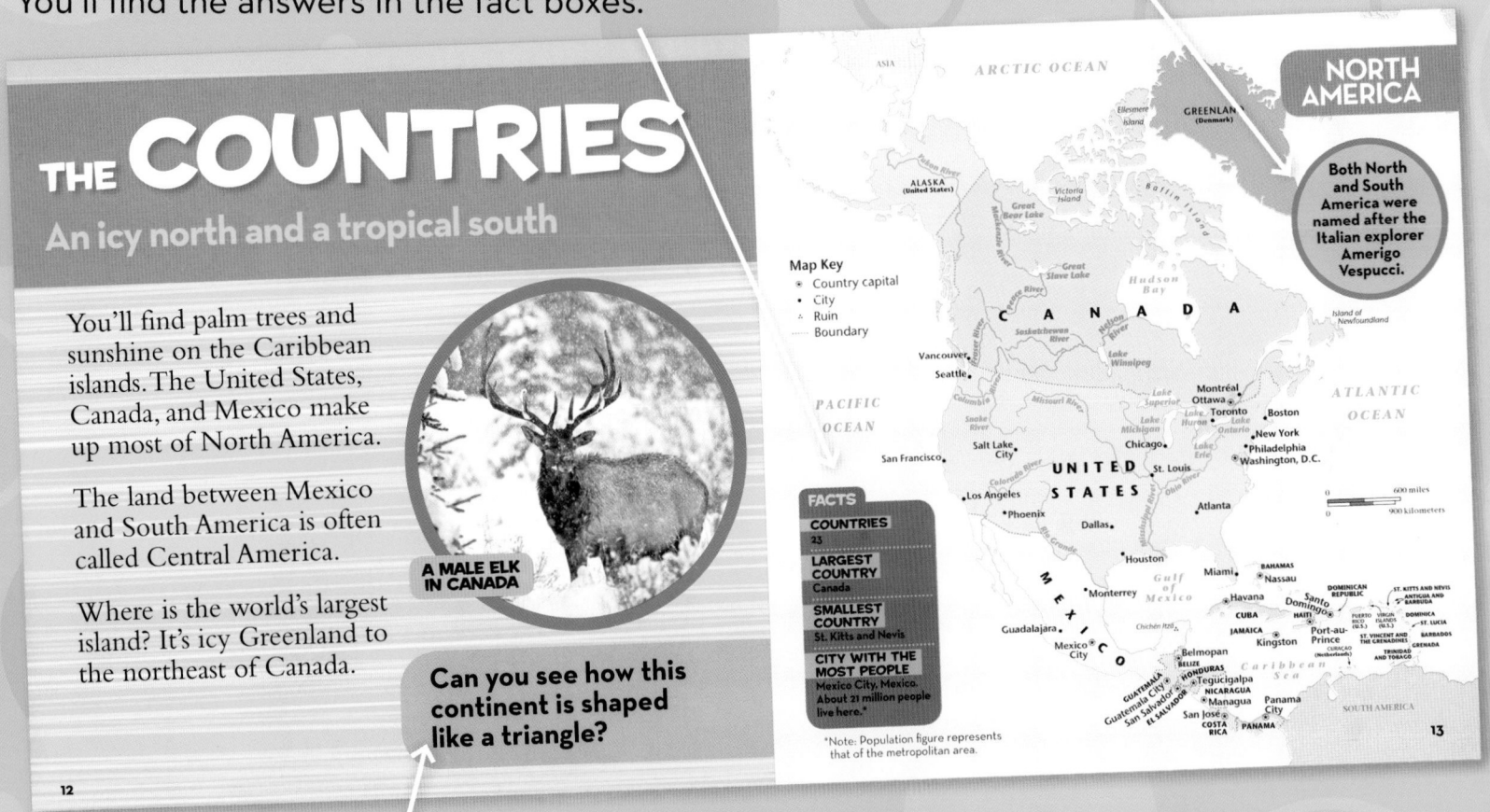

THE COUNTRIES

An icy north and a tropical south

You'll find palm trees and sunshine on the Caribbean islands. The United States, Canada, and Mexico make up most of North America.

The land between Mexico and South America is often called Central America.

Where is the world's largest island? It's icy Greenland to the northeast of Canada.

A MALE ELK IN CANADA

Can you see how this continent is shaped like a triangle?

12

NORTH AMERICA

Both North and South America were named after the Italian explorer Amerigo Vespucci.

Map Key
Country capital
City
Ruin
Boundary

FACTS
COUNTRIES
23
LARGEST COUNTRY
Canada
SMALLEST COUNTRY
St. Kitts and Nevis
CITY WITH THE MOST PEOPLE
Mexico City, Mexico. About 21 million people live here.*

*Note: Population figure represents that of the metropolitan area.

13

QUESTIONS relate the information back to you and your life. They can even start a conversation.

LET'S GO! At the end of each section you'll find activities to try, each involving art, science, math, writing, or a physical activity.

PARENT TIPS in the back of this book provide games, activities, and project ideas. Parents can use these tips to help kids make more geography connections. There's also a glossary, a list of words and their meanings.

MAP OF THE WORLD

MAPS tell you what a place is like, even if you've never been there. Maps can also help you get where you want to go. They often use drawings called **symbols** to show things. A **map key** tells you what those symbols mean.

For example, a black solid line means the boundary between countries. A black dot stands for a city. If you don't know what a symbol on a map means, check the map key.

There are two main types of maps. **Political maps** show the outlines of countries. They can also mark the location of cities and capitals. **Physical maps** are the second type of map. These maps show an area's land and water features. You can see the locations of mountain ranges, forests, deserts, plains, and bodies of water such as lakes, rivers, and oceans.

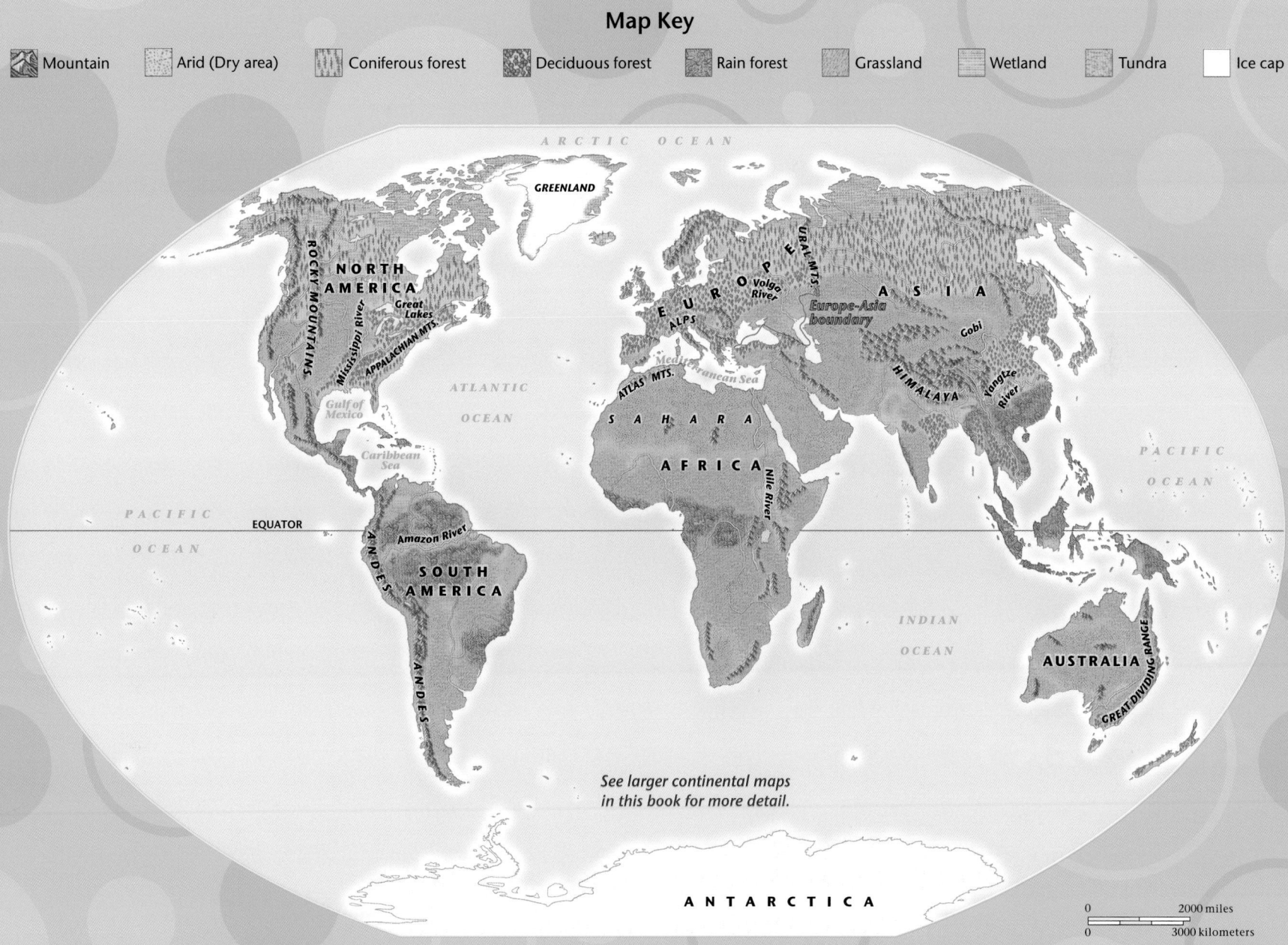

CHAPTER 1

NORTH AMERICA

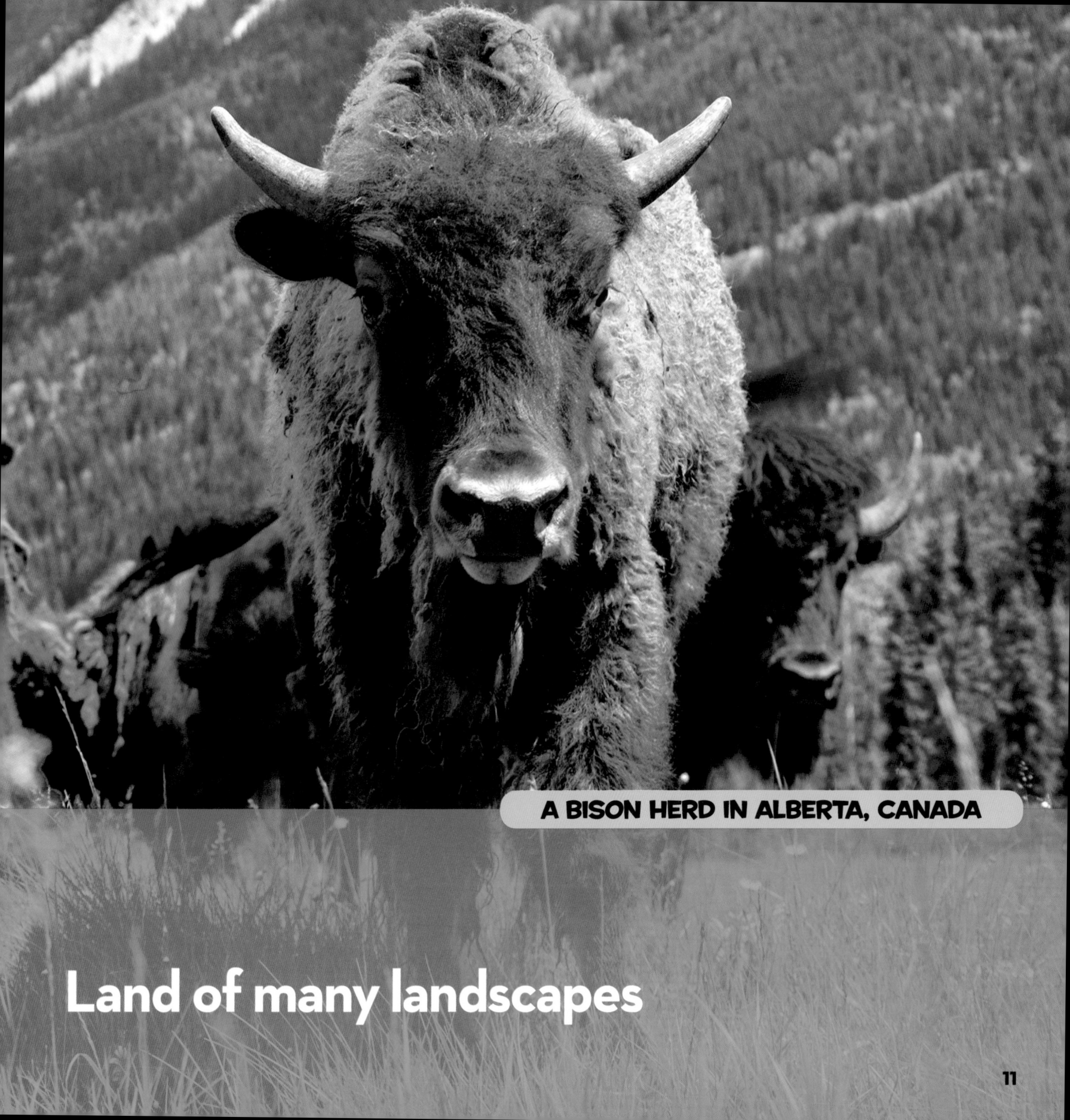

A BISON HERD IN ALBERTA, CANADA

Land of many landscapes

THE COUNTRIES

An icy north and a tropical south

You'll find palm trees and sunshine on the Caribbean islands. The United States, Canada, and Mexico make up most of North America.

The land between Mexico and South America is often called Central America.

Where is the world's largest island? It's icy Greenland to the northeast of Canada.

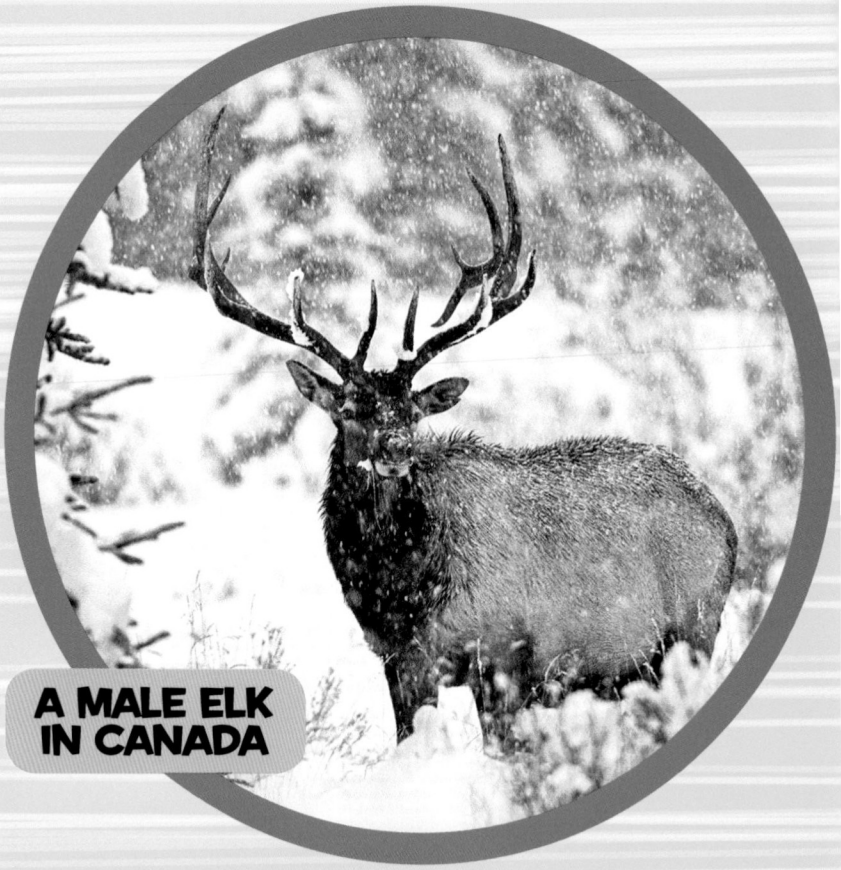

A MALE ELK IN CANADA

Can you see how this continent is shaped like a triangle?

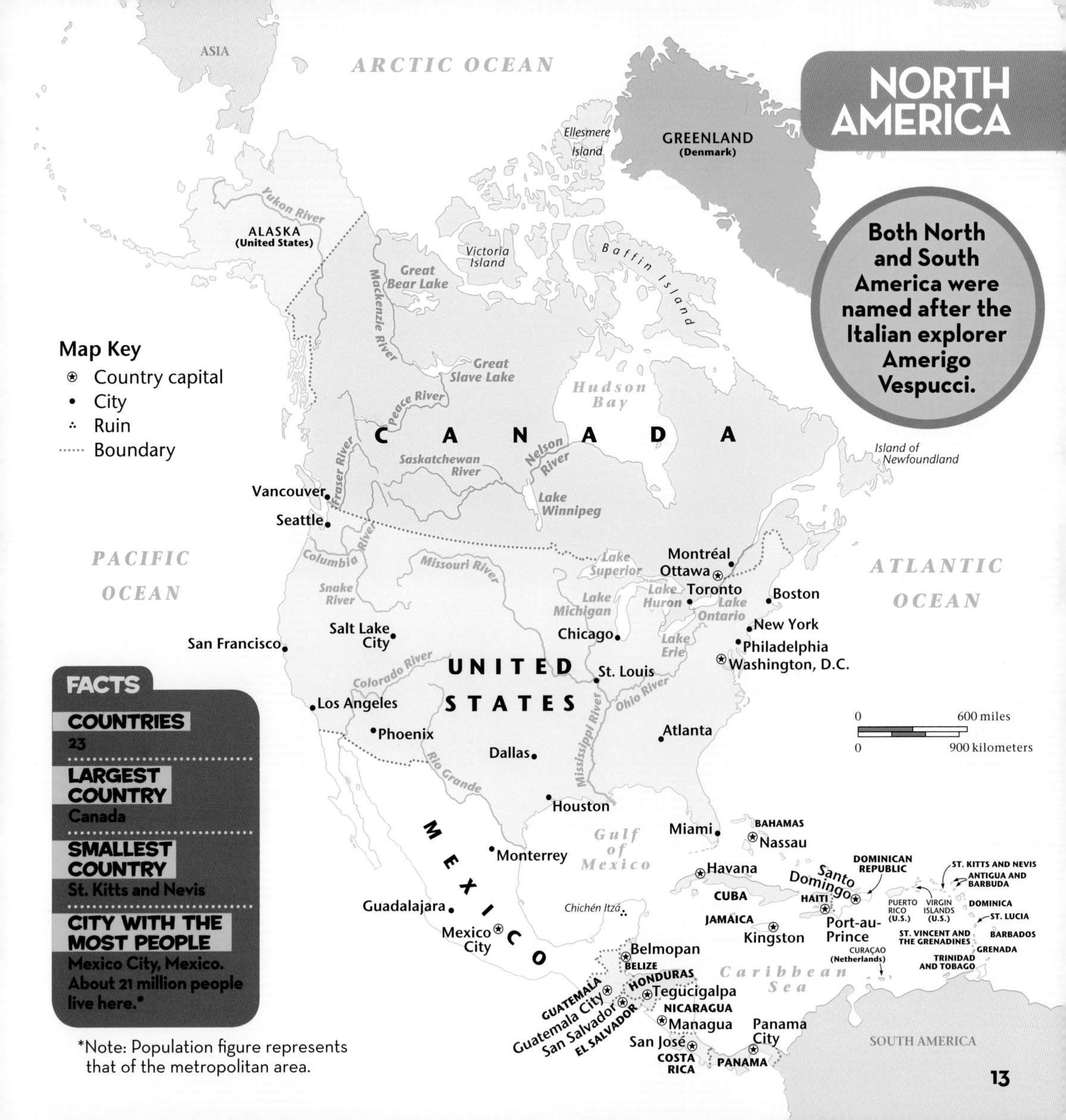
NORTH AMERICA
Both North and South America were named after the Italian explorer Amerigo Vespucci.
Map Key
Country capital
City
Ruin
Boundary
ASIA
ARCTIC OCEAN
GREENLAND (Denmark)
Ellesmere Island
ALASKA (United States)
Yukon River
Victoria Island
Baffin Island
Great Bear Lake
Mackenzie River
Great Slave Lake
Hudson Bay
Peace River
CANADA
Fraser River
Saskatchewan River
Nelson River
Island of Newfoundland
Lake Winnipeg
Vancouver
Seattle
PACIFIC OCEAN
ATLANTIC OCEAN
Columbia River
Missouri River
Lake Superior
Montréal
Ottawa
Snake River
Lake Michigan
Lake Huron
Toronto
Lake Ontario
Boston
New York
Salt Lake City
Chicago
Lake Erie
Philadelphia
San Francisco
Washington, D.C.
Colorado River
UNITED STATES
St. Louis
Ohio River
Los Angeles
Mississippi River
Phoenix
Atlanta
Dallas
Rio Grande
Houston
0 600 miles
0 900 kilometers
Miami
BAHAMAS
Nassau
MEXICO
Monterrey
Gulf of Mexico
Havana
DOMINICAN REPUBLIC
Santo Domingo
ST. KITTS AND NEVIS
ANTIGUA AND BARBUDA
CUBA
HAITI
Guadalajara
Chichén Itzá
PUERTO RICO (U.S.)
VIRGIN ISLANDS (U.S.)
DOMINICA
ST. LUCIA
JAMAICA
Port-au-Prince
Kingston
ST. VINCENT AND THE GRENADINES
BARBADOS
Mexico City
CURAÇAO (Netherlands)
GRENADA
TRINIDAD AND TOBAGO
Belmopan
BELIZE
Caribbean Sea
HONDURAS
GUATEMALA
Tegucigalpa
Guatemala City
San Salvador
EL SALVADOR
NICARAGUA
Managua
Panama City
San José
COSTA RICA
PANAMA
SOUTH AMERICA
FACTS
COUNTRIES
23
LARGEST COUNTRY
Canada
SMALLEST COUNTRY
St. Kitts and Nevis
CITY WITH THE MOST PEOPLE
Mexico City, Mexico. About 21 million people live here.*
*Note: Population figure represents that of the metropolitan area.

THE LAND

Forests cover much of North America.

Near the North Pole, the land and ocean are often frozen. The flat land in the central plains is great for farming.

KULUSUK, GREENLAND

ARCHES NATIONAL PARK, UTAH, U.S.A.

In the southwest, you'll find deserts and rocky canyons. Steamy jungles grow in the southern part of the continent.

This type of cactus can live up to 200 years!

SAGUARO CACTUS IN ARIZONA, U.S.A.

FACTS

SIZE
9,449,000 square miles (24,474,000 sq km)

HIGHEST MOUNTAIN
Mount McKinley (Denali), Alaska, U.S.A.

LOWEST PLACE
Death Valley, California, U.S.A.

LONGEST RIVER
Mississippi-Missouri River, U.S.A.

LARGEST LAKE
Lake Superior, U.S.A. and Canada

More tornadoes form in the United States than anywhere else on Earth.

A BEACH IN TULUM, MEXICO

THE WEATHER

Hot in the south, chilly in the north

In the south, it's warm year-round, and many days are sunny!

Farther north, seasons bring cool autumn weather and rainy springs. It's cold all the time in the northernmost part of the continent. The ground is always frozen.

THE PEOPLE

People from all over the world have moved here.

GIRLS IN GUATEMALA

More than 8,000 years ago, people from Asia made their way across a land bridge to North America. More recently, people from all over the world have settled here. That's why North America has many different cultures.

People celebrate where they're from with parades, festivals, and sporting events.

Basketball was invented in North America in 1891.

A BASKETBALL GAME IN PENNSYLVANIA, U.S.A.

Kids go tobogganing (a type of sledding) in Nunavut, Canada's northernmost territory.

NUNAVUT, CANADA

MOTHER AND BABY POLAR BEARS

Manatees have fingernails on their front flippers.

THE ANIMALS

From musk oxen to manatees

Many types of animals live in North America. Some, like musk oxen and polar bears, are built for the cold. You can find manatees in waters of the warm south.

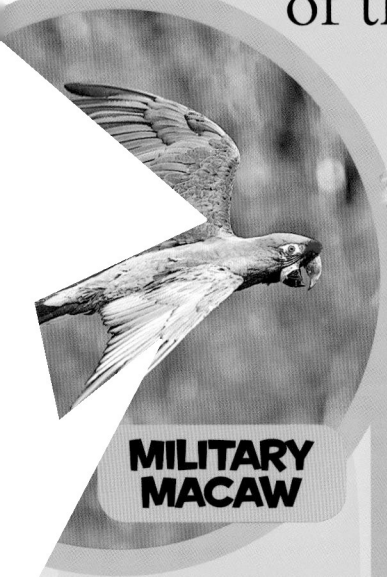

MILITARY MACAW

SQUIRREL MONKEY

MUSK OX

Parrots and monkeys squawk and screech in the rain forests of Central America.

THE SIGHTS

Old stone pyramids and a monumental gift

GRAND CANYON, U.S.A.

North America has many natural wonders, like the Grand Canyon. There are man-made ones, too.

CHICHÉN ITZÁ, MEXICO

The Maya people of Mexico and northern Central America built great stone pyramids long ago. These pyramids still stand today.

NORTH AMERICA

The Statue of Liberty stands in New York Harbor. France gave it to the United States as a gift.

The Statue of Liberty stands 305 feet (93 m) tall.

A symbol most people aren't able to see: Lady Liberty has a broken chain wrapped around her feet. It stands for the freedom that people find in the United States.

LET'S GO!

Sing in three languages

Most North Americans speak Spanish, English, or French. Try singing "Frère Jacques" in the three primary languages of North America.

Fray Felipe
(Spanish)

Fray Felipe, Fray Felipe,
¿Duermes tú? ¿Duermes tú?
¡Suenan las campanas!
¡Suenan las campanas!
Ding, dang, dong. Ding, dang, dong.

Frère Jacques
(French)

Frère Jacques, Frère Jacques,
Dormez-vous? Dormez-vous?
Sonnez les matines! Sonnez les matines!
Ding, dang, dong. Ding, dang, dong.

Brother John
(English)

Are you sleeping, are you sleeping,
Brother John? Brother John?
Morning bells are ringing!
Morning bells are ringing!
Ding, dang, dong.
Ding, dang, dong.

CHAPTER 2

SOUTH AMERICA

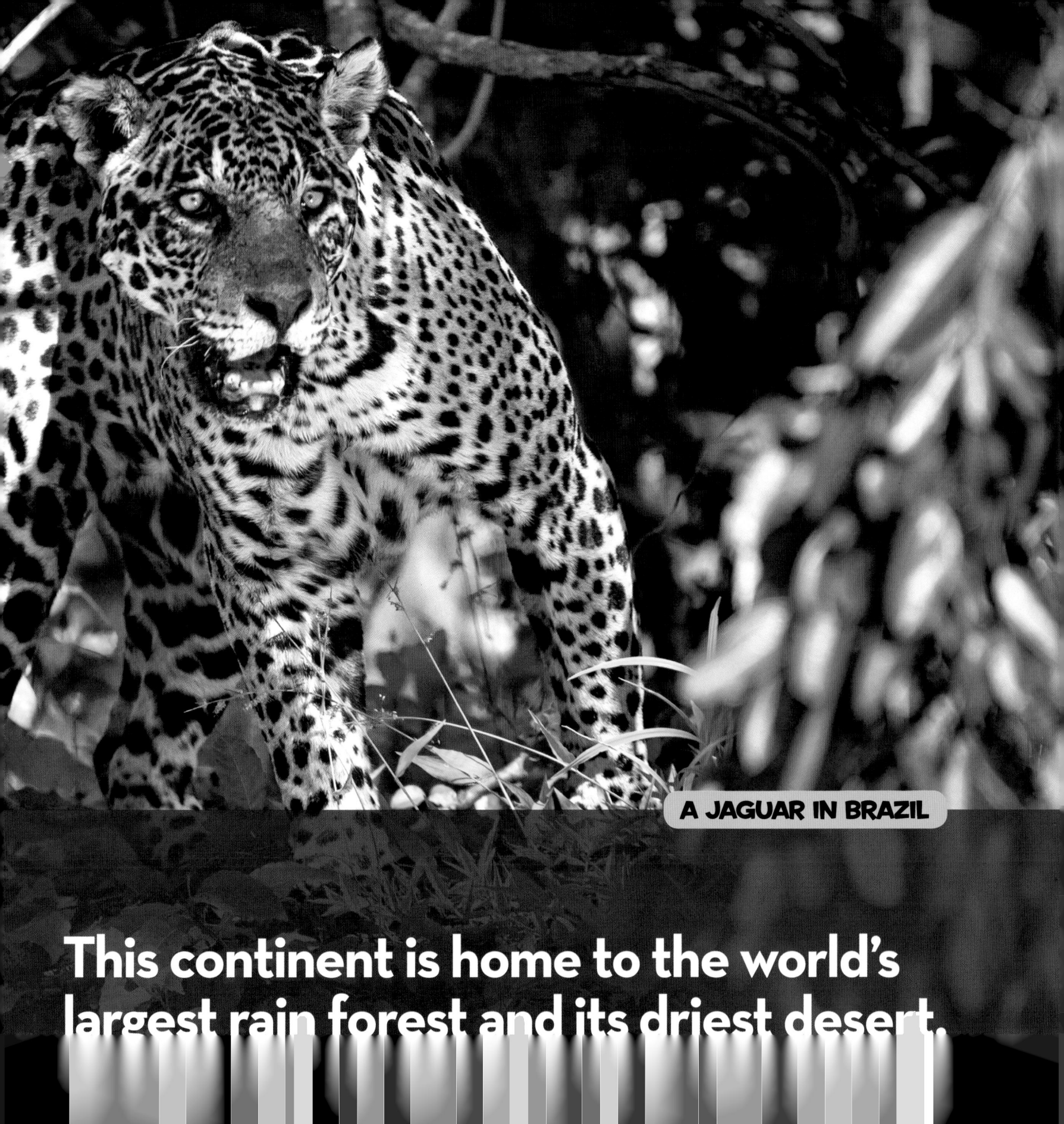

A JAGUAR IN BRAZIL

This continent is home to the world's largest rain forest and its driest desert.

THE COUNTRIES

From big Brazil to small Suriname

South America has 12 countries. Farming is important here.

Many foods come from this continent. Potatoes, tomatoes, and bananas are a few.

Most big cities are near the coasts.

A BEACH IN RIO DE JANEIRO, BRAZIL

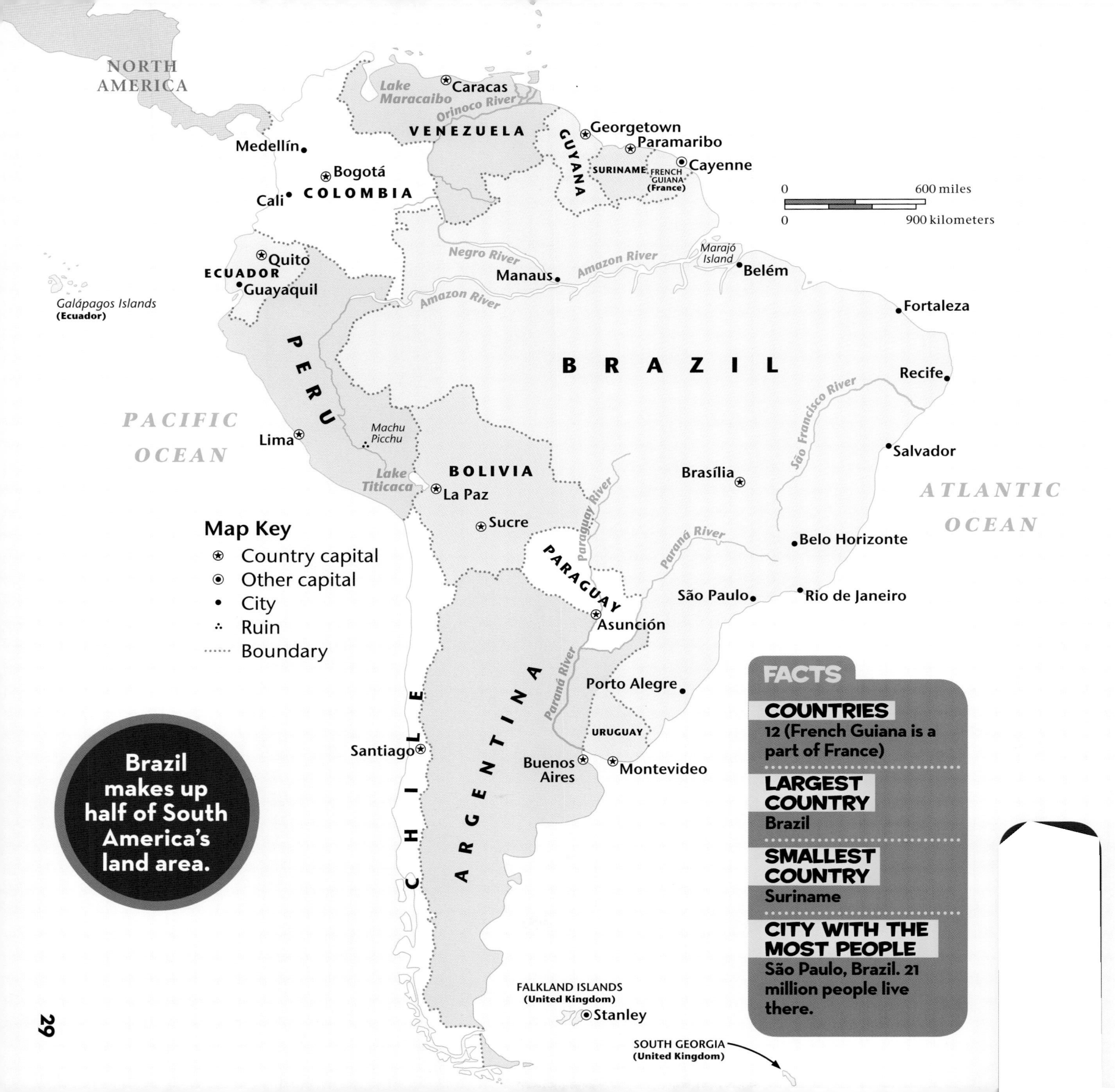

Brazil makes up half of South America's land area.

FACTS

COUNTRIES
12 (French Guiana is a part of France)

LARGEST COUNTRY
Brazil

SMALLEST COUNTRY
Suriname

CITY WITH THE MOST PEOPLE
São Paulo, Brazil. 21 million people live there.

THE LAND

The world's longest mountain range and its second longest river are here.

The Andes mountain range stretches down the west side of South America. Some of these mountains are volcanoes!

The Amazon River is very long. It snakes through the Amazon rain forest.

AMAZON RIVER

Parts of the Atacama Desert haven't seen a drop of rain since people began keeping weather records 400 years ago!

The Atacama Desert in Chile is the driest place on Earth.

LOS FLAMENCOS NATIONAL RESERVE, CHILE

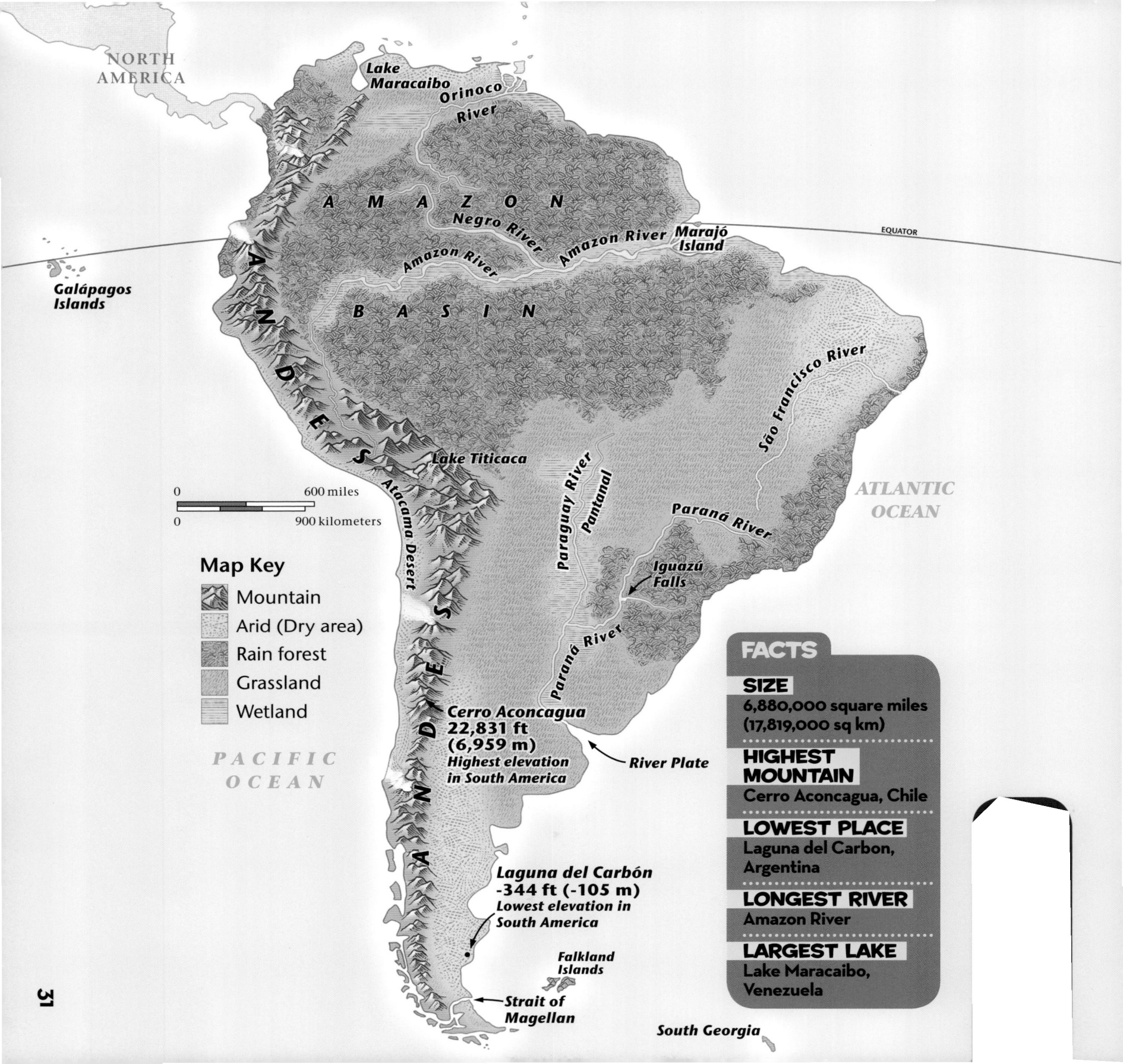
NORTH AMERICA
Lake Maracaibo
Orinoco River
A M A Z O N
Negro River
Amazon River
Amazon River
Marajó Island
EQUATOR
Galápagos Islands
B A S I N
A N D E S
São Francisco River
Lake Titicaca
Atacama Desert
Paraguay River
Pantanal
Paraná River
ATLANTIC OCEAN
0 600 miles
0 900 kilometers
Iguazú Falls
Map Key
Mountain
Arid (Dry area)
Rain forest
Grassland
Wetland
Paraná River
PACIFIC OCEAN
Cerro Aconcagua
22,831 ft
(6,959 m)
Highest elevation in South America
River Plate
Laguna del Carbón
-344 ft (-105 m)
Lowest elevation in South America
Falkland Islands
Strait of Magellan
South Georgia
FACTS
SIZE
6,880,000 square miles (17,819,000 sq km)
HIGHEST MOUNTAIN
Cerro Aconcagua, Chile
LOWEST PLACE
Laguna del Carbon, Argentina
LONGEST RIVER
Amazon River
LARGEST LAKE
Lake Maracaibo, Venezuela

The ice fields at Glaciers National Park in Argentina are the largest outside of Antarctica.

GLACIERS NATIONAL PARK, PATAGONIA, ARGENTINA

THE WEATHER

Rain forest bound? Bring your umbrella!

It's hot and rainy in the northern half of South America. The Amazon rain forest is here. Parts of the forest get up to nine feet (2.7 m) of rain a year.

The southern tip of South America is very cold. That's because it's so far away from the Equator. Giant ice sheets cover some parts of the land there.

TUMUCUMAQUE NATIONAL PARK, BRAZIL

THE PEOPLE

Olá! Hola! That's how most people say "hello" in South America.

PERUVIAN GIRL

Very long ago, people made their way from Asia across North America into South America. Over time, they built great cities. People from Europe and Africa came later.

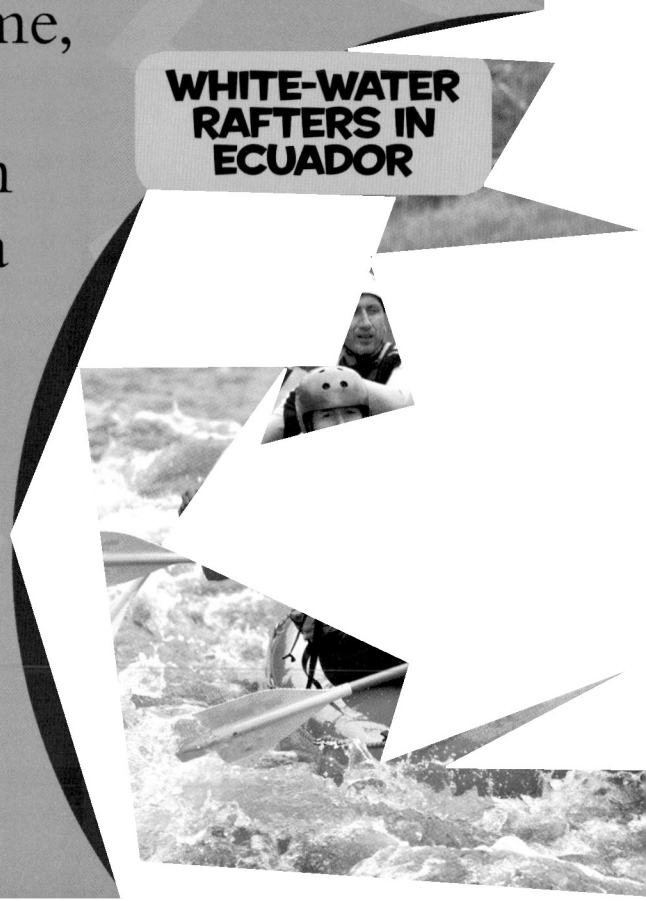

WHITE-WATER RAFTERS IN ECUADOR

Today, most South Americans are related to Asian, European, or African groups. Portuguese and Spanish are the main languages.

SOUTH AMERICA

Soccer is the most popular sport in South America. Goal!

Guanacos are related to camels. They live on the plains, plateaus, and coastlines of Peru, Chile, and Argentina. They also live in the Andes.

A type of parrot, the blue-and-yellow macaw has a powerful beak for cracking nuts and seeds.

THE ANIMALS

Critters in a rainbow of colors

A wide variety of animals live in South America. There are blue-and-yellow macaws, poison dart frogs, and pink river dolphins in the rain forest.

POISON DART FROG

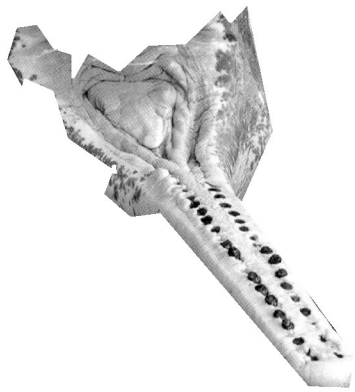

PINK RIVER DOLPHIN

You'll find llamas in the mountains. Armadillos live in different areas of the continent.

THE SIGHTS

Hiking boots and dancing shoes

Travelers hike a long way to see stone ruins on a mountaintop in Peru. The site is called Machu Picchu. It's known as the Lost City of the Inca. The Inca were ancient South American people.

A CARNIVAL FESTIVAL

Many South Americans celebrate Carnival. It's a festive season, usually in February. In Rio de Janeiro, Brazil, people wear colorful costumes and dance in the streets.

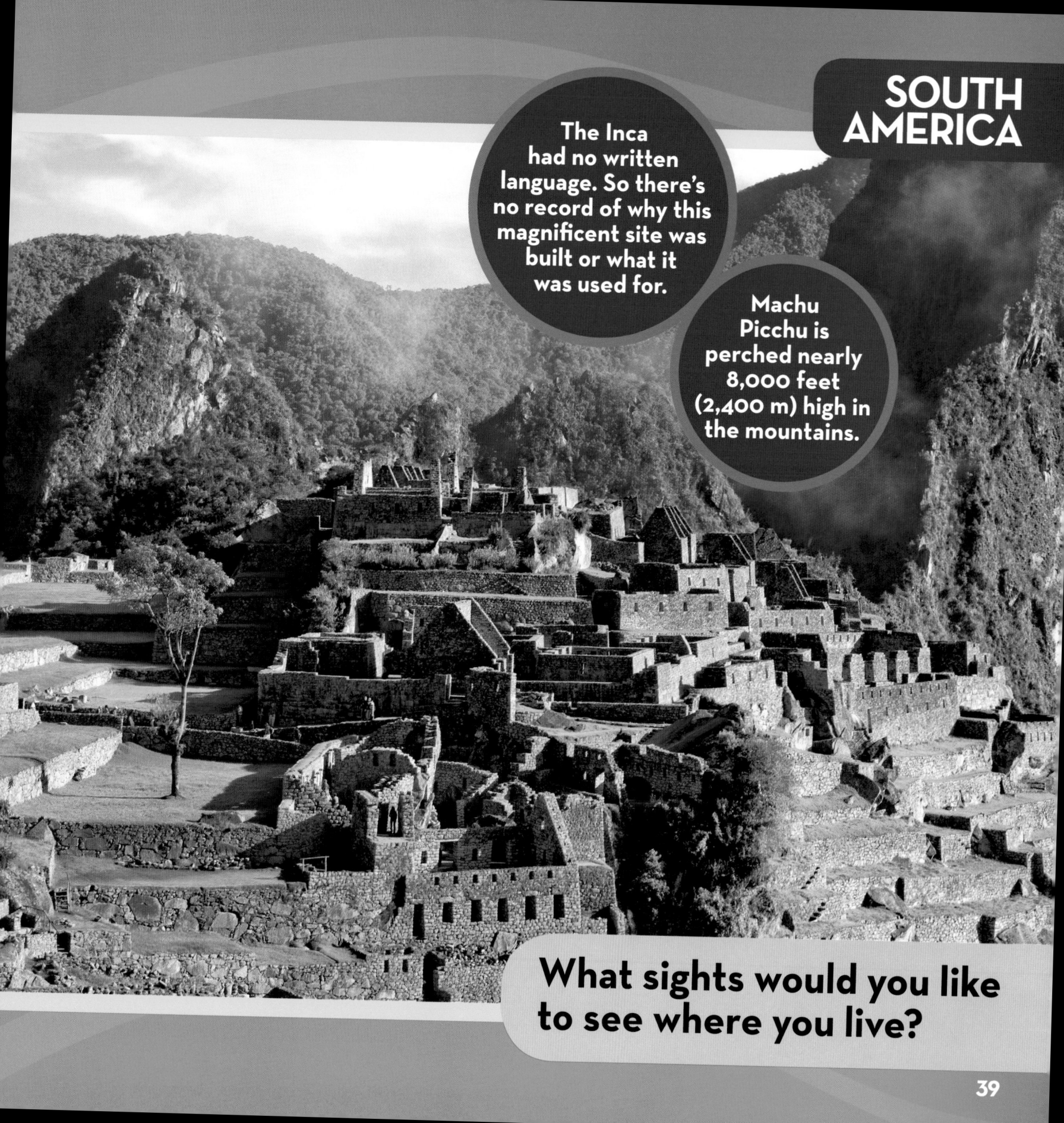

The Inca had no written language. So there's no record of why this magnificent site was built or what it was used for.

Machu Picchu is perched nearly 8,000 feet (2,400 m) high in the mountains.

What sights would you like to see where you live?

LET'S GO!

Make a rain forest

You'll need:

- a clean 2-liter soda bottle
- scissors
- tape
- small stones or pebbles
- potting soil
- plants that like moisture (moss, spider plants, or miniature ferns work well)
- water
- decorative rocks, animal figures, bits of bark (optional)

1

Ask an adult to cut off the top part of the bottle. Save the top. Use tape to cover the sharp edge.

2

Sprinkle a thin layer of pebbles over the bottom of the bottle.

3

Fill the bottle a little more than halfway with soil. Make a small hole in the soil for the plants.

4

Place the plants in the hole. Fill around them with soil.

5

To make your rain forest look more realistic, add some pebbles, rocks, animal figures, or bits of bark.

6

Water the plants by dampening the soil. Don't overwater.

7

Tape the top back onto the bottle, leaving the cap off. Place the rain forest in a bottle in a sunny spot.

CHAPTER 3
EUROPE

THE CITY OF LONDON, ENGLAND

Where old meets new

THE COUNTRIES

Countries of all sizes

Europe is the second smallest continent. But it has lots of countries. Many of the major cities are on the coasts or along Europe's long rivers.

Russia's lands stretch from Europe into Asia. Since Russia's major cities are in Europe, it's counted as a European country.

FACTS

COUNTRIES
46

LARGEST COUNTRY
Russia

SMALLEST COUNTRY
Vatican City

CITY WITH THE MOST PEOPLE
Moscow, Russia. 12 million people live there.

ST. BASIL'S CATHEDRAL, MOSCOW, RUSSIA

The name Europe comes from Europa, a princess in Greek mythology.
Barents Sea
Norwegian Sea
North Sea
Baltic Sea
Black Sea
Caspian Sea
Mediterranean Sea
Shetland Islands
Orkney Islands
NORWAY
SWEDEN
FINLAND
RUSSIA
EUROPE-ASIA BOUNDARY
Oslo
Stockholm
Helsinki
St. Petersburg
Tallinn
ESTONIA
LATVIA
Riga
Moscow
DENMARK
Copenhagen
LITHUANIA
KALININGRAD (Russia)
Vilnius
Minsk
BELARUS
NETHERLANDS
Amsterdam
Hamburg
Brussels
BELGIUM
Berlin
GERMANY
Rhine River
Warsaw
POLAND
Volga River
KAZAKHSTAN
Volgograd
Paris
LUXEMBOURG
Prague
CZECH REPUBLIC
Kraków
Kiev
UKRAINE
Danube River
SLOVAKIA
Bern
SWITZERLAND
LIECHTENSTEIN
Vienna
Bratislava
AUSTRIA
Budapest
HUNGARY
MOLDOVA
Chişinău
Rhône R.
SLOVENIA
Ljubljana
Zagreb
CROATIA
ROMANIA
CRIMEA
Belgrade
Bucharest
SAN MARINO
BOSNIA AND HERZEGOVINA
SERBIA
Sarajevo
GEORGIA
Tbilisi
Baku
AZERBAIJAN
MONACO
ITALY
MONTENEGRO
Kosovo
Pristina
BULGARIA
Sofia
Corsica (France)
VATICAN CITY
Rome
Podgorica
Skopje
MACEDONIA
NAXCIVAN (Azerbaijan)
Tirana
Naples
ALBANIA
Istanbul
Ankara
Sardinia (Italy)
GREECE
TURKEY
ASIA
Sicily
Athens
Valletta
MALTA
Crete
NORTHERN CYPRUS
Nicosia
CYPRUS
Map Key
Country capital
City
Boundary
Disputed territory shown in light gray

THE LAND

Long rivers and curvy coastlines

Europe has a lot of coastline. It wraps around many different types of bodies of water.

There are bays, seas, and gulfs. Long rivers crisscross the continent. People have used these waterways to trade goods for thousands of years.

FACTS

SIZE
3,841,000 square miles (9,947,000 sq km)

HIGHEST MOUNTAIN
El'brus, Russia

LOWEST PLACE
Caspian Sea

LONGEST RIVER
Volga River, Russia

LARGEST LAKE
Lake Ladoga, Russia

Can you spot Europe's four major rivers? They're the Rhine, the Danube, the Rhône, and the Volga.

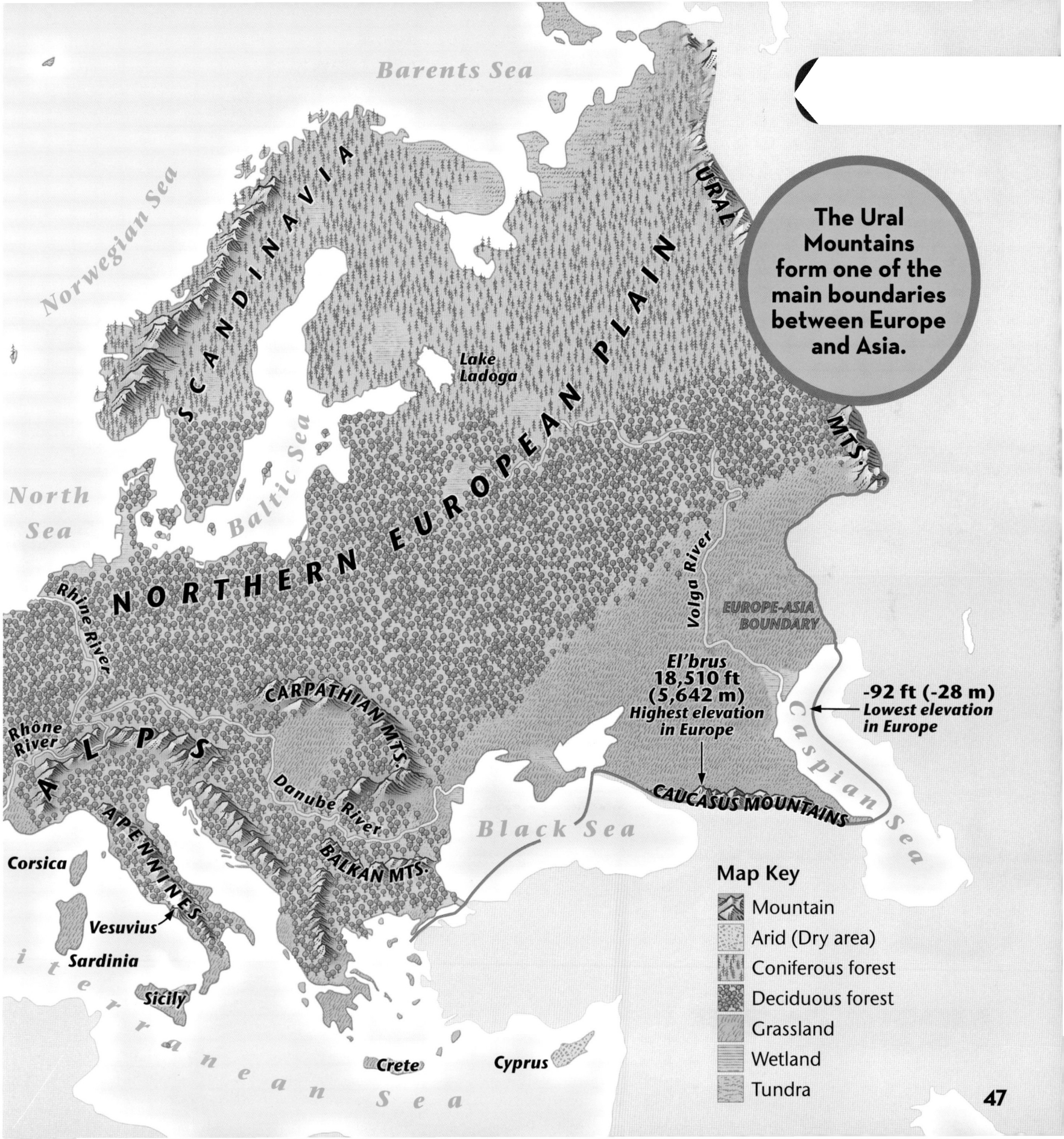

The Ural Mountains form one of the main boundaries between Europe and Asia.

BLACK FOREST IN GERMANY

A BEACH ON THE GREEK ISLAND OF CRETE

THE WEATHER

Mostly mild with plenty of rain

Warm winds blow over Europe from the Atlantic Ocean. This gives much of the continent mild weather. The land is good for farming and raising animals.

Near the Mediterranean Sea, it's warm and sunny all year-round. In the far north, it can get very cold during winter.

SHEEP IN ARCOS DE LA FRONTERA, SPAIN

THE PEOPLE

Many countries, many languages

AN ICELANDIC GIRL WITH HER LAMB

There are many different groups of people living in Europe. More than 50 languages are spoken here. That's more than one per country!

Europe has a long history. The land was once divided among many kingdoms and empires.

Children in Switzerland often study three languages in school—German, English, and French or Italian.

Imagine going to school in a gondola! If you could ride to school in any way, how would you do it?

GONDOLAS IN VENICE, ITALY

This eagle owl is one of the world's largest owl species.

Owls are expert hunters. Some can even take on larger prey such as foxes, opossums, and hares.

THE ANIMALS

Feathery owls and feisty squirrels

Many animals make their homes in the forests of Europe. Rabbits, squirrels, and owls are common.

ALPINE MARMOT

Reindeer and caribou are the same animal! They are known as reindeer in Europe and caribou in North America.

REINDEER

Otters snack on fish in the streams and lakes. In the north, you can find reindeer and arctic fox. Alpine marmots dig winter burrows in the slopes of the Alps.

THE SIGHTS

Stepping into history

People who lived long ago built many of the famous places throughout Europe. Stonehenge is a circle of arranged rocks in England. People built it more than 4,000 years ago. It may have helped them study the stars.

THE COLOSSEUM IN ROME, ITALY

Ancient Romans packed Rome's Colosseum to watch events such as gladiator fights.

STONEHENGE IN ENGLAND

Disneyland's Sleeping Beauty Castle is modeled after Neuschwanstein Castle in Germany.

Castles were once the homes of kings and other wealthy people. One small town in Italy had 72 castles at one time!

EXPLORER SPOTLIGHT

Carsten Peter visits explosive volcanoes.

Carsten Peter wears a heatproof suit. He follows scientists into the mouth of Mount Etna. It's one of the world's most active volcanoes. Mount Etna is on the island of Sicily in Italy.

Carsten's job is to take pictures of an eruption. He joins scientists as they study erupting volcanoes. The scientists want to gather samples of the melted rock, or lava. It's dangerous work. The temperature can climb to 2000°F (1093°C). Dangerous gases fill the air.

Why take the risks? Because no one knows when volcanoes will pop. Explosions can be deadly for the people living near a volcano's slopes. Information from these studies can help save lives.

LET'S GO!

Be an artist like Michelangelo

Michelangelo was a famous European artist. He painted the ceiling of the Sistine Chapel in Vatican City 500 years ago. The paintings are some of the most famous European artworks. Create your own masterpiece the way Michelangelo did! Ask for an adult's help and permission first.

1

Ask an adult to help you set up your art project.

You'll need:

- large sheet(s) of paper
- tape
- crayons, colored pencils, or washable markers
- kitchen table or card table

3

Pretend you're painting the ceiling like Michelangelo. Draw your own scene on the paper.

4

Take down the paper and admire your masterpiece.

CHAPTER 4
ASIA

THE TAJ MAHAL IN AGRA, INDIA

The world's largest continent

THE COUNTRIES

Lots of land, lots of people

Everything seems bigger in Asia. More people live here than anywhere else on Earth. You'll find the most crowded cities here. Shanghai in China is home to 24 million people.

The city of Tokyo in Japan has the world's busiest metro train system.

FACTS

COUNTRIES
46

LARGEST COUNTRY
China

SMALLEST COUNTRY
Maldives

CITY WITH THE MOST PEOPLE
Tokyo, Japan. 38 million people live there.

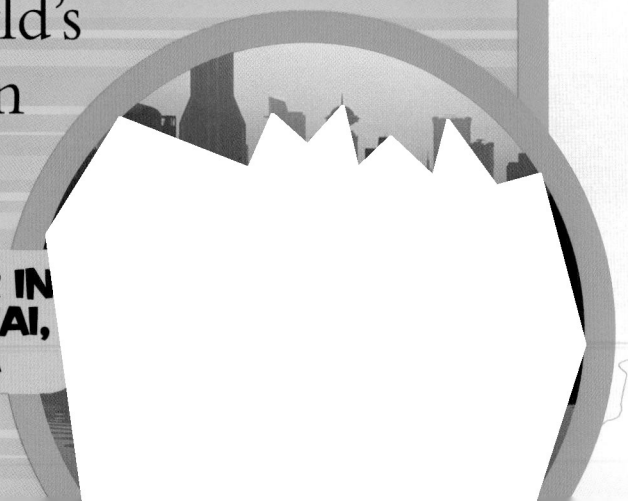

A FISHER IN SHANGHAI, CHINA

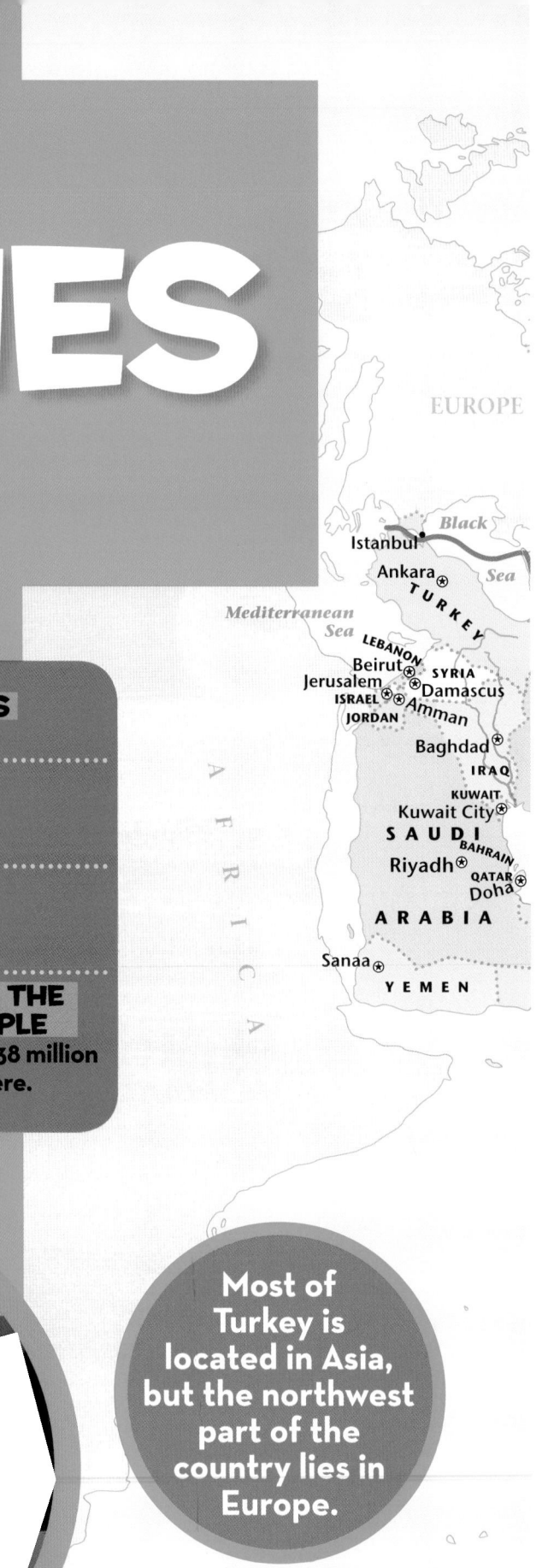

Most of Turkey is located in Asia, but the northwest part of the country lies in Europe.

NORTH AMERICA
NORTH AMERICA
ARCTIC OCEAN
Bering Sea
New Siberian Islands
North Land
Novaya Zemlya
Baltic Sea
RUSSIA
EUROPE-ASIA BOUNDARY
Moscow
R U S S I A
Ob River
Yenisey River
Lena River
Sakhalin
Irtysh River
Amur River
Lake Baikal
GEORGIA
Tbilisi
ARMENIA
Yerevan
AZERBAIJAN
Baku
Caspian Sea
Astana
KAZAKHSTAN
UZBEKISTAN
TURKMENISTAN
Ashgabat
Tashkent
Bishkek
KYRGYZSTAN
Dushanbe
TAJIKISTAN
Tehran
IRAN
AFGHANISTAN
Kabul
Islamabad
Indus River
Persian Gulf
Abu Dhabi
UNITED ARAB EMIRATES
Muscat
OMAN
PAKISTAN
Karachi
Delhi
New Delhi
Ulaanbaatar
MONGOLIA
Harbin
Shenyang
Beijing
NORTH KOREA
Pyongyang
Seoul
SOUTH KOREA
JAPAN
Tokyo
Yokohama
TOKYO, JAPAN
Yellow River
Xi'an
C H I N A
Shanghai
PACIFIC OCEAN
Wuhan
Chengdu
Yangtze River
Chongqing
Taipei
TAIWAN
Brahmaputra River
Mekong River
NEPAL
Kathmandu
Thimphu
BHUTAN
Ganges River
BANGLADESH
Dhaka
Kolkata (Calcutta)
Hong Kong
Hanoi
Hainan
MYANMAR (BURMA)
LAOS
Vientiane
Arabian Sea
Mumbai (Bombay)
INDIA
Nay Pyi Taw
Yangon (Rangoon)
THAILAND
VIETNAM
Bay of Bengal
Bangkok
CAMBODIA
Phnom Penh
Ho Chi Minh City
South China Sea
PHILIPPINES
Manila
Philippine Sea
Chennai (Madras)
Colombo
SRI LANKA
Sri Jayewardenepura Kotte
MALDIVES
Male
Bandar Seri Begawan
BRUNEI
MALAYSIA
Kuala Lumpur
SINGAPORE
Sumatra
Borneo
Celebes
New Guinea
I N D O N E S I A
Díli
TIMOR-LESTE (EAST TIMOR)
Jakarta
Java
Bali
INDIAN OCEAN
AUSTRALIA
Map Key
Country capital
Other capital
City
Boundary
Disputed territory shown in light gray
0 600 miles
0 900 kilometers

THE LAND

Rooftop of the world

You'll find ten of the world's tallest mountain peaks in Asia. They're all in one large mountain chain called the Himalaya.

Rain forests and green valleys appear south of these mountains. The land is frozen for most of the year in the north. Thirsty deserts make up most of central Asia.

MOUNT EVEREST, CHINA-NEPAL BORDER

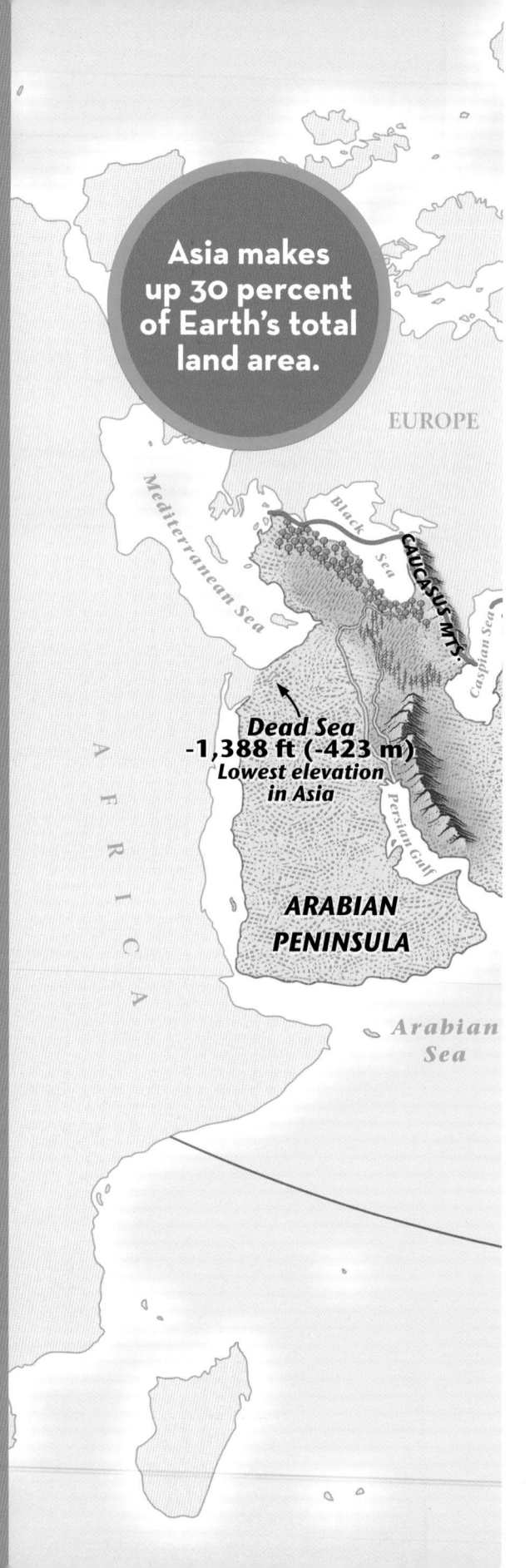

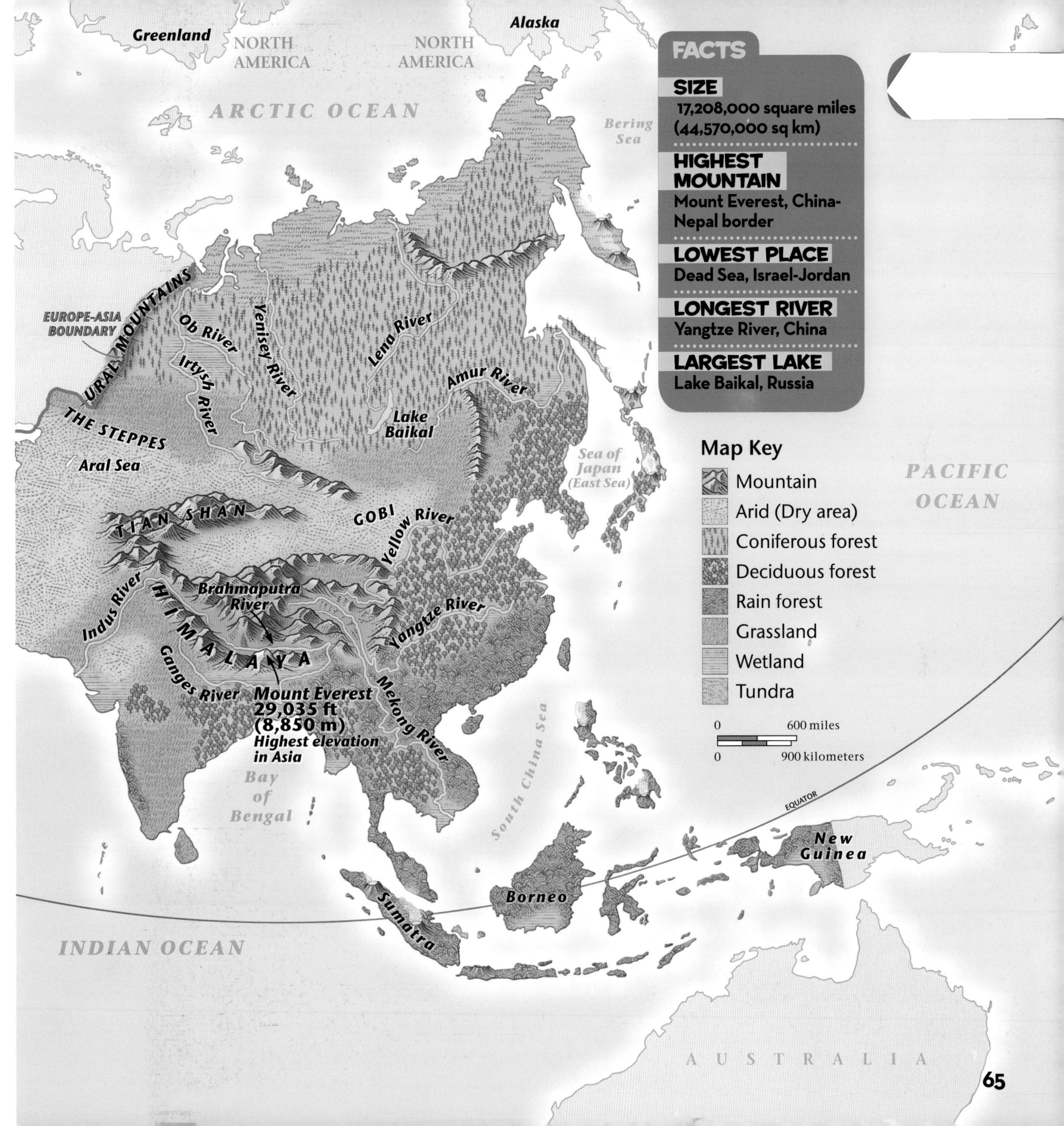
Greenland
NORTH AMERICA
NORTH AMERICA
Alaska
ARCTIC OCEAN
Bering Sea
EUROPE-ASIA BOUNDARY
URAL MOUNTAINS
Ob River
Yenisey River
Lena River
Irtysh River
Amur River
Lake Baikal
THE STEPPES
Aral Sea
Sea of Japan (East Sea)
PACIFIC OCEAN
TIAN SHAN
GOBI
Yellow River
Indus River
HIMALAYA
Brahmaputra River
Yangtze River
Ganges River
Mount Everest
29,035 ft
(8,850 m)
Highest elevation in Asia
Mekong River
South China Sea
Bay of Bengal
EQUATOR
New Guinea
Borneo
Sumatra
INDIAN OCEAN
AUSTRALIA
FACTS
SIZE
17,208,000 square miles (44,570,000 sq km)
HIGHEST MOUNTAIN
Mount Everest, China-Nepal border
LOWEST PLACE
Dead Sea, Israel-Jordan
LONGEST RIVER
Yangtze River, China
LARGEST LAKE
Lake Baikal, Russia
Map Key
Mountain
Arid (Dry area)
Coniferous forest
Deciduous forest
Rain forest
Grassland
Wetland
Tundra
0 600 miles
0 900 kilometers

RIDING THROUGH THE RAIN IN VIETNAM

THE GOBI IN MONGOLIA DURING WINTER

A TEA PLANTATION IN MALAYSIA

Northern Asia has long, icy winters and short, cool summers. It rarely rains in the deserts in Asia's central and western parts.

In the south, heavy rains soak the land in the summer. The rains allow farmers to grow water-loving crops like rice.

A RICE PADDY

Most of the world's rice is grown in Asia.

THE PEOPLE

Land of many traditions

KIDS AT SCHOOL IN THAILAND

Many different groups of people live in Asia. They each have their own language and culture. Some traditions are very old.

The world's first cities were built here thousands of years ago.

WAITING FOR A BUS IN INDIA

Millions of people visit Mecca, Saudi Arabia, every year for a religious journey. The tradition is part of the Muslim faith and is called a hajj. It's the world's largest gathering.

RIMAGE
ECCA IN
DI ARABIA

What are your family's favorite traditions?

A Bengal tiger's roar can be heard up to two miles (3 km) away.

Fuzzy pandas live only in the bamboo forests of China.

THE ANIMALS

Lizards, tigers, and bears!

Tigers prowl the forests of India and some other parts of Asia. The world's largest lizard lives in Asia. It's called the Komodo dragon.

KOMODO DRAGON

YAK

Woolly yaks live high up in the Himalaya.

THE SIGHTS

Ancient temples, super skyscrapers, and a great wall

Temples and the ruins of old cities can be found throughout Asia. Angkor Wat in Cambodia is a huge temple that was built over 900 years ago.

THE GREAT WALL OF CHINA

China's Great Wall is the largest structure built by humans. It was built in sections over hundreds of years. The wall is 13,000 miles (20,921 km) long!

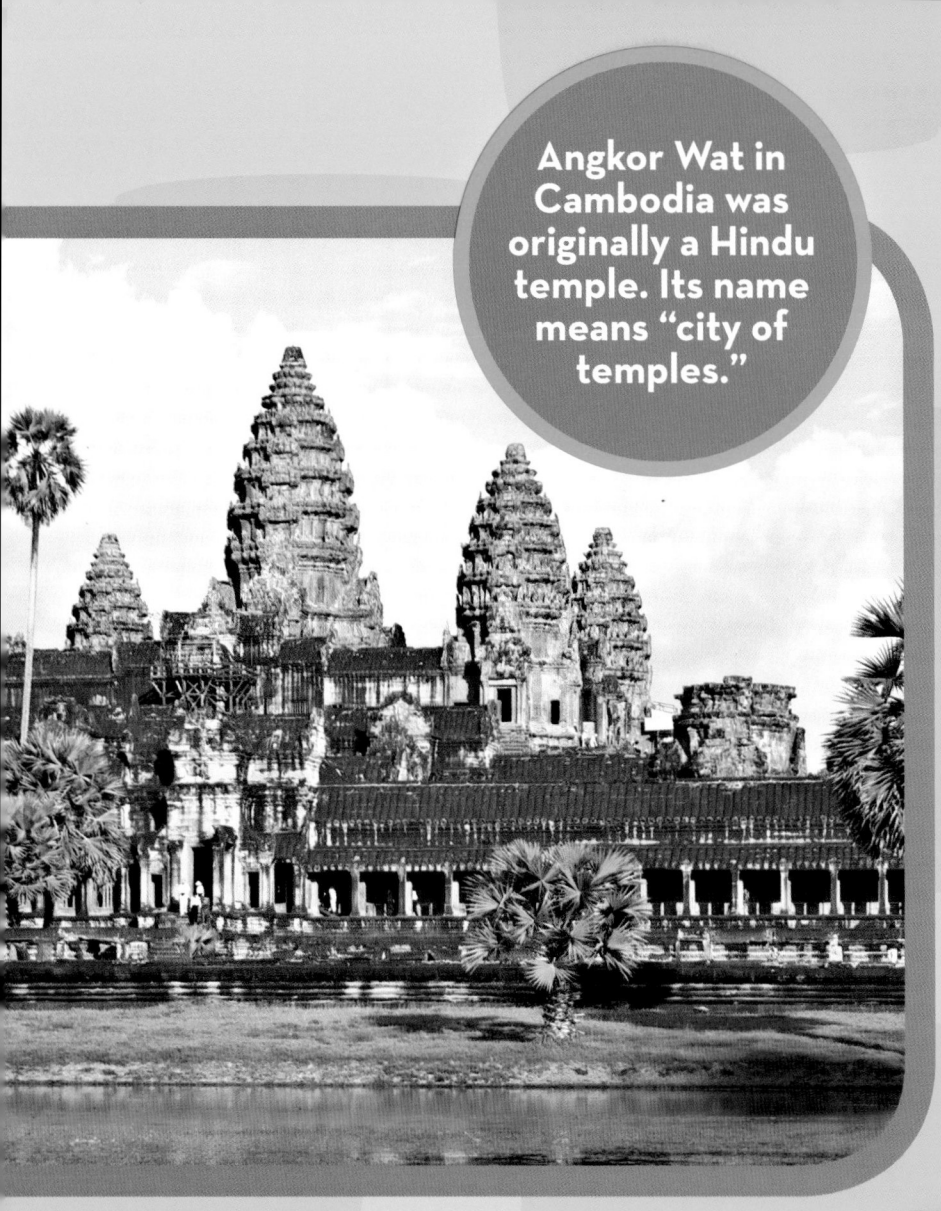

Angkor Wat in Cambodia was originally a Hindu temple. Its name means "city of temples."

THE BURJ KHALIFA BUILDING

Burj Khalifa in the United Arab Emirates is a new marvel. It's the world's tallest skyscraper. It's as tall as nine Statues of Liberty stacked on top of each other.

LET'S GO!

Design a mosaic

Some sites in Asia are famous for their mosaics. These beautiful, patterned tiles decorate places like the Blue Mosque in Turkey and the Taj Mahal in India. You can make your own mosaic!

You'll need:

- pencil
- ruler
- scissors
- colored construction paper cut into a variety of shapes, such as triangles, diamonds, pentagons, squares (Draw the shapes on the paper first. Make sure that each shape is the same size and that you have enough of each to make a repeating pattern.)
- 3 or more pieces of cardboard
- glue

ASIA
1
Arrange the pattern blocks or shapes on one cardboard square. Once you're happy with the design, glue the shapes to the square. This is one "tile."
2
You can make as many tiles as you like.
3
Put the tiles together. Count how many different shapes you used in your mosaic. Which shape did you use the most?

CHAPTER 5
AFRICA

A HERD OF ELEPHANTS IN KENYA

Life on the move

ost of an

Of all the continents, Africa is divided into the most countries.

The newest country is South Sudan. It was created in 2011.

Africa has 18,500 miles (30,000 km) of coastline.

A boy carries a tray of fresh bread through busy streets in Cairo, Egypt.

Some cities are very crowded. But most Africans live in smaller villages and farms.

FACTS

COUNTRIES
54

LARGEST COUNTRY
Algeria

SMALLEST COUNTRY
Seychelles

CITY WITH THE MOST PEOPLE
Cairo, Egypt. 18 million people live there.

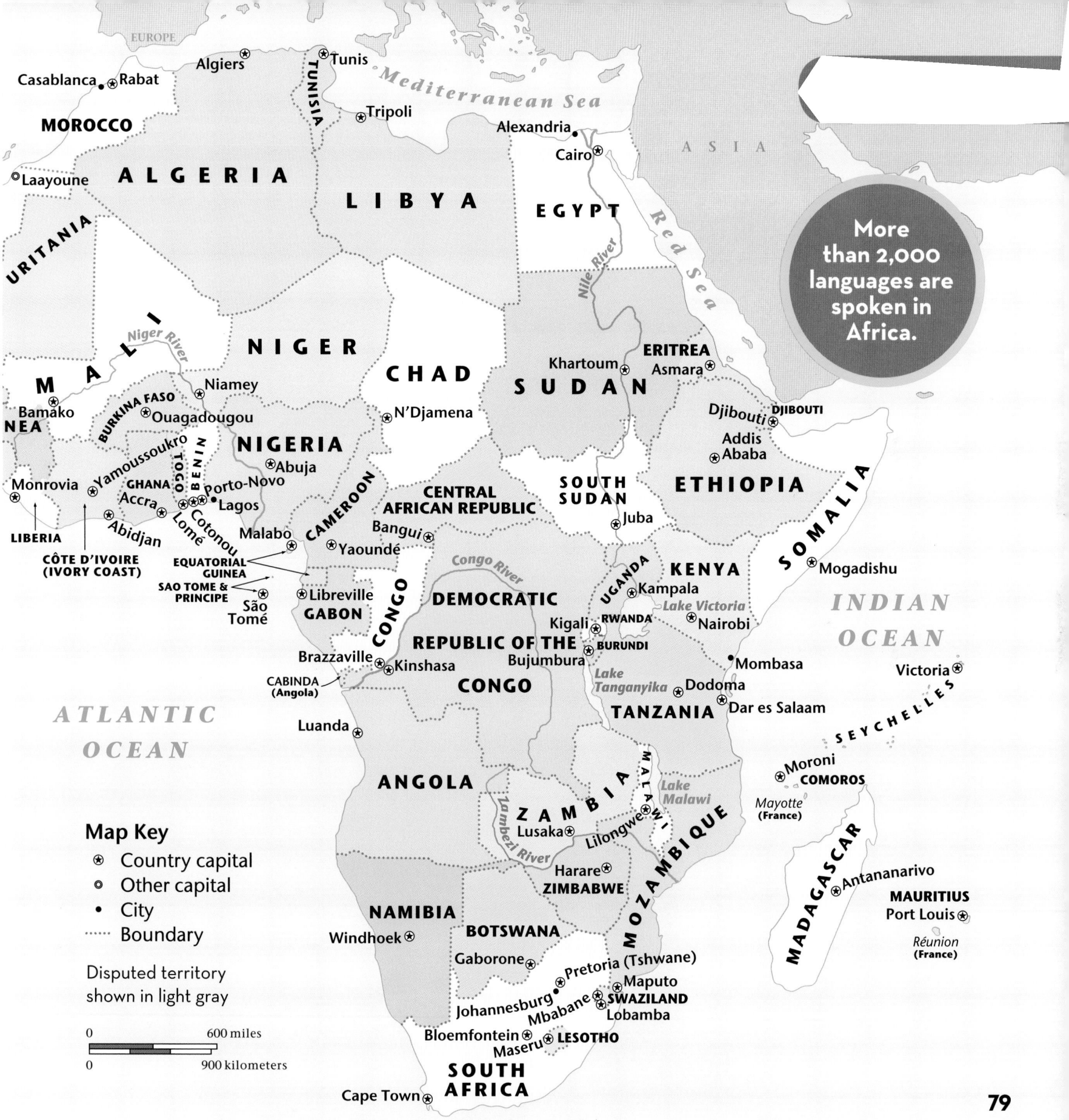
More than 2,000 languages are spoken in Africa.
EUROPE
ASIA
Mediterranean Sea
Red Sea
Casablanca
Rabat
Algiers
Tunis
TUNISIA
Tripoli
MOROCCO
Alexandria
Cairo
Laayoune
ALGERIA
LIBYA
EGYPT
URITANIA
Nile River
Niger River
MALI
NIGER
CHAD
SUDAN
Khartoum
ERITREA
Asmara
Bamako
Niamey
BURKINA FASO
Ouagadougou
N'Djamena
Djibouti
DJIBOUTI
Addis Ababa
NIGERIA
Abuja
Monrovia
Yamoussoukro
GHANA
Accra
TOGO
BENIN
Porto-Novo
Lagos
Lomé
Cotonou
CAMEROON
CENTRAL AFRICAN REPUBLIC
SOUTH SUDAN
ETHIOPIA
SOMALIA
Juba
LIBERIA
Abidjan
CÔTE D'IVOIRE (IVORY COAST)
Malabo
Bangui
Yaoundé
EQUATORIAL GUINEA
SAO TOME & PRINCIPE
São Tomé
Libreville
GABON
Congo River
CONGO
DEMOCRATIC REPUBLIC OF THE CONGO
UGANDA
Kampala
KENYA
Mogadishu
Lake Victoria
Nairobi
Kigali
RWANDA
BURUNDI
Bujumbura
INDIAN OCEAN
Brazzaville
Kinshasa
CABINDA (Angola)
Mombasa
Victoria
Lake Tanganyika
Dodoma
TANZANIA
Dar es Salaam
SEYCHELLES
ATLANTIC OCEAN
Luanda
ANGOLA
Moroni
COMOROS
Mayotte (France)
ZAMBIA
Lusaka
Lambezi River
MALAWI
Lake Malawi
Lilongwe
MOZAMBIQUE
Harare
ZIMBABWE
MADAGASCAR
Antananarivo
MAURITIUS
Port Louis
Réunion (France)
NAMIBIA
Windhoek
BOTSWANA
Gaborone
Pretoria (Tshwane)
Maputo
Johannesburg
Mbabane
SWAZILAND
Lobamba
Bloemfontein
Maseru
LESOTHO
SOUTH AFRICA
Cape Town
Map Key
Country capital
Other capital
City
Boundary
Disputed territory shown in light gray
0
600 miles
0
900 kilometers

THE LAND

Dry deserts in the north and south, lush forests in the middle

Most of Africa is on a high, flat plateau. There aren't many mountains here. Most craggy peaks are in the east.

You'll find deserts at the northern and southern parts of Africa. A band of forests and grasslands called savannas make up the middle.

ZEBRAS IN TANZANIA

FACTS

SIZE
11,608,000 square miles (30,065,000 sq km)

HIGHEST MOUNTAIN
Kilimanjaro, Tanzania

LOWEST PLACE
Lake Assal, Djibouti

LONGEST RIVER
Nile River

LARGEST LAKE
Lake Victoria

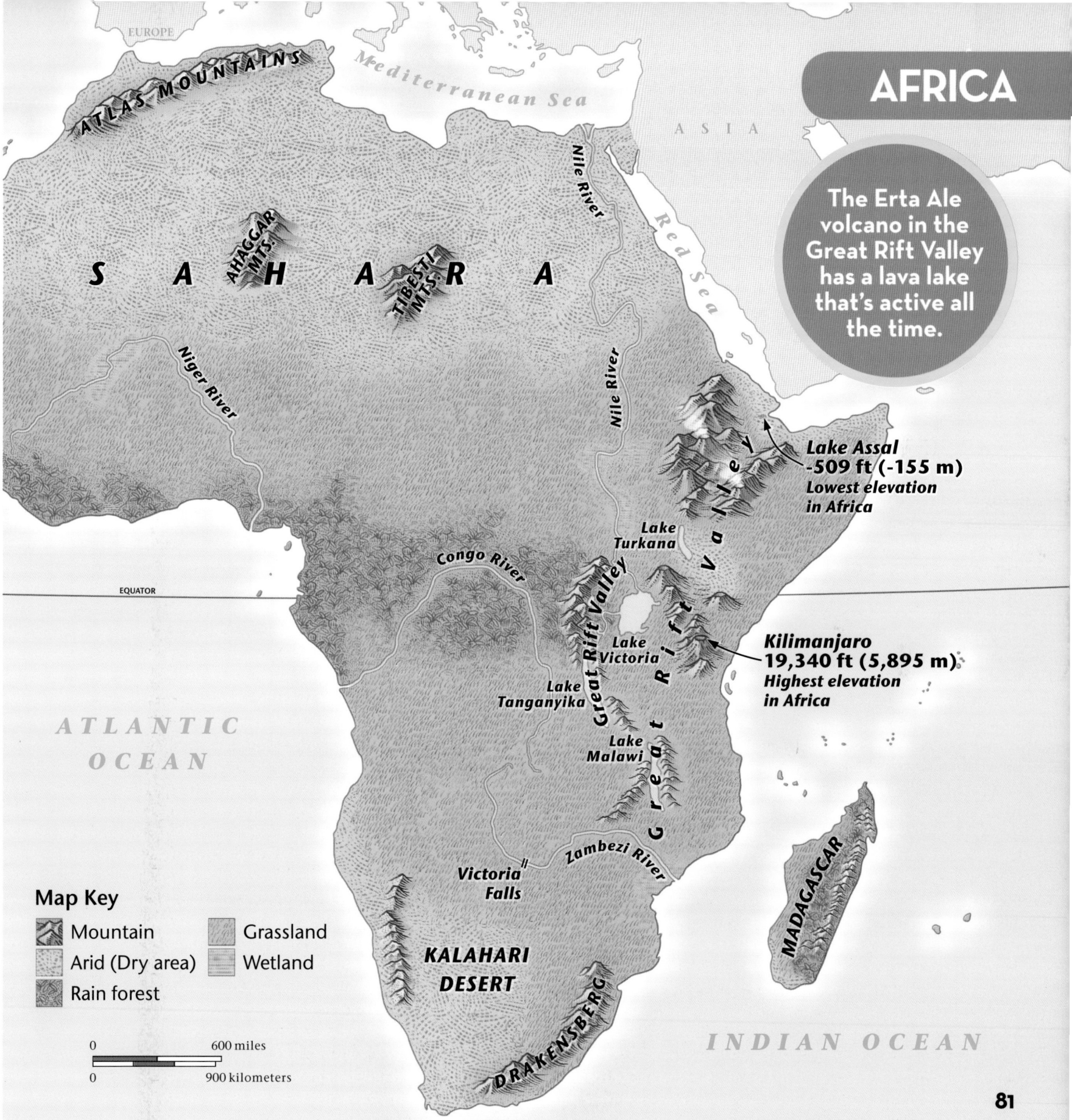
AFRICA
The Erta Ale volcano in the Great Rift Valley has a lava lake that's active all the time.
EUROPE
Mediterranean Sea
ASIA
ATLAS MOUNTAINS
Nile River
Red Sea
AHAGGAR MTS.
SAHARA
TIBESTI MTS.
Niger River
Nile River
Lake Assal
-509 ft (-155 m)
Lowest elevation in Africa
Great Rift Valley
Lake Turkana
Congo River
EQUATOR
Great Rift Valley
Lake Victoria
Kilimanjaro
19,340 ft (5,895 m)
Highest elevation in Africa
Lake Tanganyika
ATLANTIC OCEAN
Lake Malawi
Great Rift Valley
Zambezi River
Victoria Falls
MADAGASCAR
KALAHARI DESERT
DRAKENSBERG
INDIAN OCEAN
Map Key
Mountain
Arid (Dry area)
Rain forest
Grassland
Wetland
0
600 miles
0
900 kilometers

A RAIN FOREST IN UGANDA

KILIMANJARO, TANZANIA

THE WEATHER

Dry, hot, and rainy

Most places in Africa are very hot. The continent doesn't have any cold-weather environments. It's rainy in the middle of Africa. You'll find rain forests there. North Africa contains the world's largest hot desert—the Sahara.

CAMEL CARAVAN IN THE SAHARA

Strong winds in the Sahara can cause sand storms.

How would you stay cool in the desert?

THE PEOPLE

Our ancient origins

NAIROBI, KENYA

People have lived in Africa longer than any other place. Scientists think that humans came from here.

STUDENTS IN SWAZILAND

Today, many groups of people live in Africa. Some focus on farming and herding. Others live in booming cities where there are lots of businesses.

Masai houses are usually circular or star-shaped.

MASAI CHILDREN IN FRONT OF A MUD HUT, MASAI MARA, KENYA

The giraffe is Earth's tallest animal.
HIPPOPOTAMUS

IMALS

for a safari!

Africa is famous for its animal life. You'll find herds of elephants, prides of lions, and towers of giraffes.

A MOTHER LION AND HER CUBS

GORILLA

In the forests of central Africa, gorillas munch peacefully on leaves.

Hungry hippos wade through the rivers and lakes.

THE SIGHTS

Pyramids, wildlife, and waterfalls

Visitors are awed by Egypt's Great Sphinx and pyramids. The ancient Egyptians built them 4,500 years ago.

GREAT PYRAMID AT GIZA, EGYPT

Every zebra has its own unique stripe pattern.

Animal lovers go to the grasslands to see Africa's great animal herds.

Victoria Falls is one of Africa's natural wonders. Its African name means "smoke that thunders." The falls create mist that can be spotted from more than 12 miles (19 km) away.

EXPLORER SPOTLIGHT

Jane Goodall uncovers the world of chimpanzees.

In 1960, Jane Goodall traveled to Africa, packing a pair of binoculars and a notebook. She wanted to learn everything she could about chimpanzees. These apes are humans' closest animal relatives.

Jane lived near chimps in the forests and went to watch them every day. She observed their behavior and took notes. She made many new discoveries. Her work turned into one of the longest studies of chimpanzee behavior.

The descendants of the chimps Jane studied in the 1960s still live in Gombe National Park.

LET'S GO!

Watch animals like a scientist

Jane Goodall made important discoveries about animals by simply watching them. Make a field guide of animal life in your neighborhood.

1 Take your supplies into your backyard or on a walk through your neighborhood. (Get an adult's permission first.)

You'll need:

- notebook
- pen or pencil
- colored pencils (optional)
- binoculars (optional)

3

Try to do your observations at the same time each day, or once a week. Write down any changes that take place.

4

After a few weeks or months, go back and look at your notes. Do you notice any changes happening over time?

5

Continue your observations for as long as you like!

CHAPTER 6

AUSTRALIA

A RING-TAILED DRAGON LIZARD IN SHARK BAY, AUSTRALIA

The land down under

THE COUNTRIES

Australia is a country and a continent in one.

Australia is the smallest of the seven continents. It makes up just 5 percent of Earth's land.

It is the only continent that is also a country. It is made up of six states. Australia is called "the land down under" because the whole country is south of, or "under," the Equator.

BLUE-WINGED KOOKABURRA

FACTS

COUNTRIES
1

STATE WITH THE MOST PEOPLE
New South Wales

STATE WITH THE FEWEST PEOPLE
Tasmania

CITY WITH THE MOST PEOPLE
Sydney. 4.5 million people live there.

A

WESTERN AUSTRALIA

INDIAN OCEAN

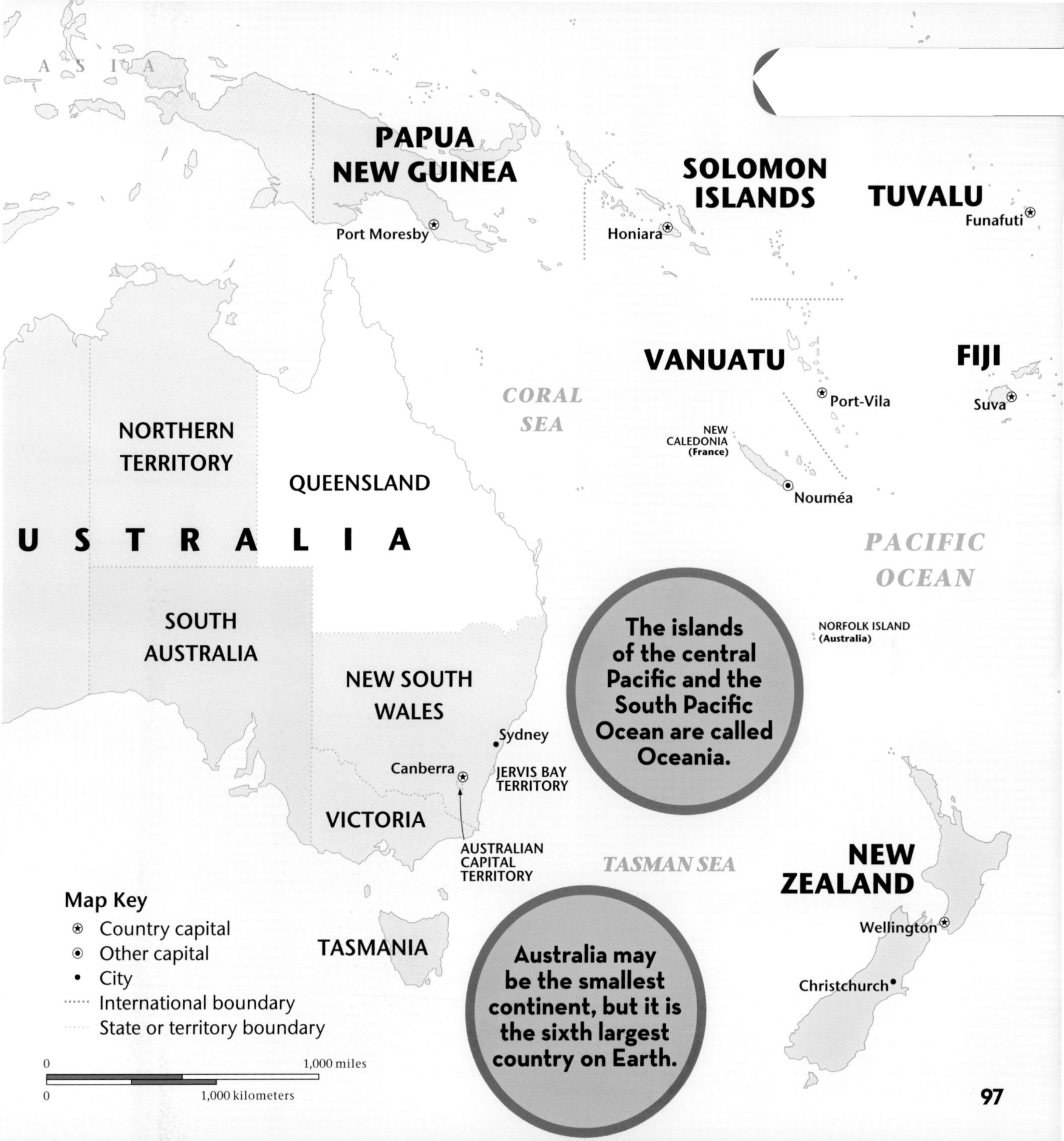

The islands of the central Pacific and the South Pacific Ocean are called Oceania.

Australia may be the smallest continent, but it is the sixth largest country on Earth.

THE LAND

A dry and flat
thousands of

A mountain range runs down Australia's east coast. It blocks rain from the Pacific Ocean. The rest of the continent is dry and flat. The interior is nicknamed the outback.

ULURU

Eucalyptus and acacia trees are the most common plants found in Australia. Tasmania has large areas of rain forests and mountains.

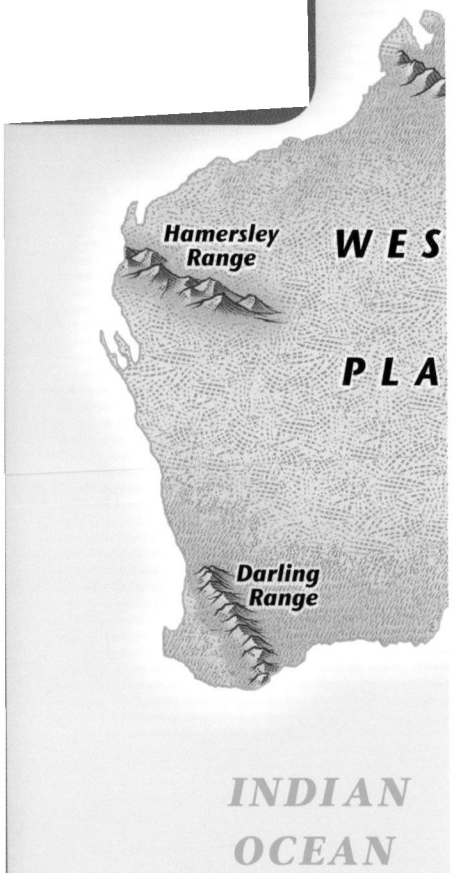

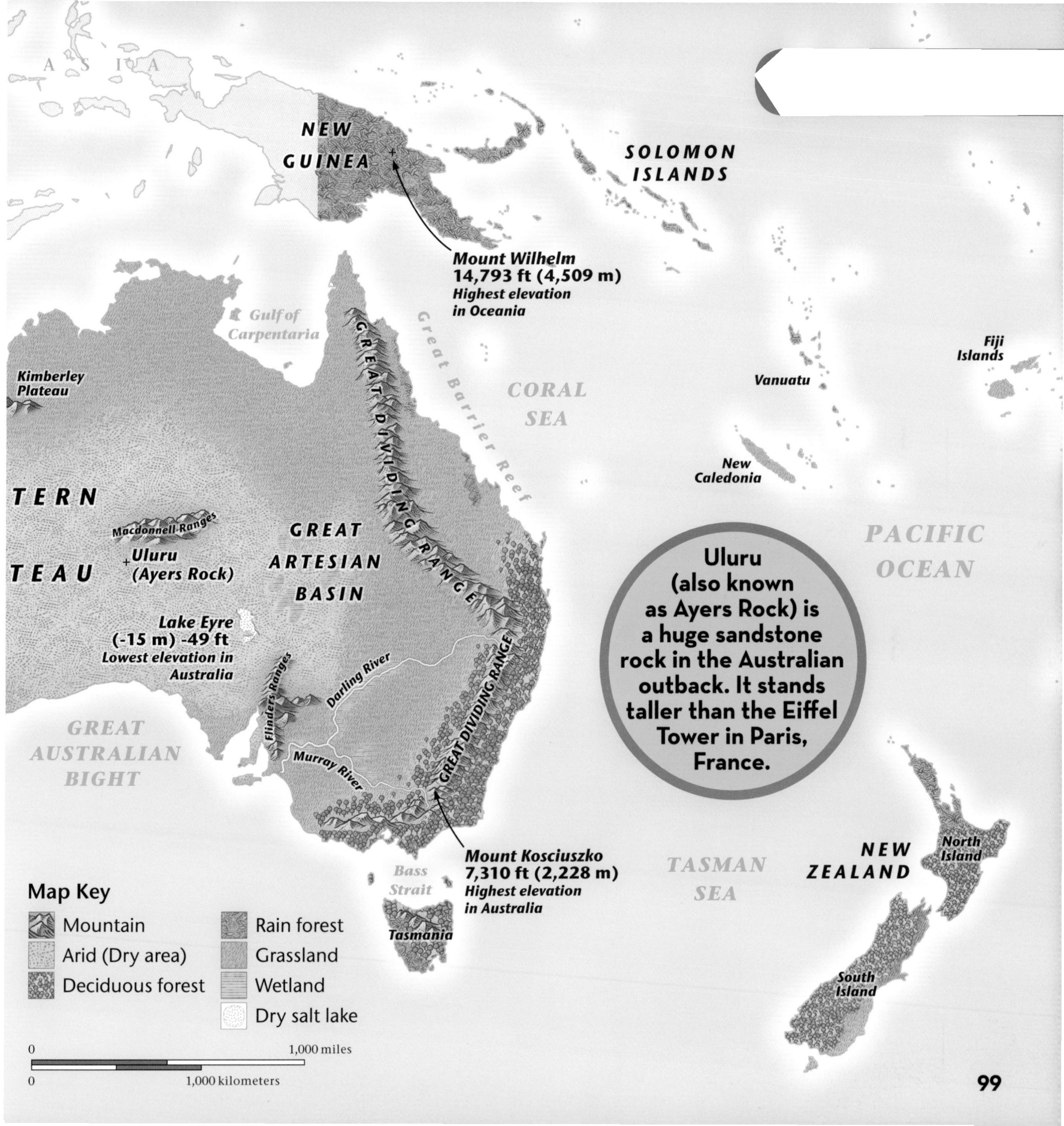

Uluru (also known as Ayers Rock) is a huge sandstone rock in the Australian outback. It stands taller than the Eiffel Tower in Paris, France.

LIMESTONE ROCK TOWERS IN THE AUSTRALIAN DESERT

MILLAA MILLAA FALLS IN QUEENSLAND, AUSTRALIA

THE WEATHER

Sunscreen is a must!

Most of Australia is warm and sunny all the time. Ocean winds bring rain to the coasts. This causes thick forests to grow in some areas.

Hurricanes are a summer weather threat in the region. In this part of the world, hurricanes have a different name. They are called cyclones.

A STORM OVER SYDNEY HARBOR

THE PEOPLE

Ocean crossers on the move

Aboriginals first came to Australia from Asia about 40,000 years ago. They have one of the world's oldest cultures. Storytelling, painting, and dance are all important parts of their lives.

ABORIGINAL GIRLS WITH FACE PAINT

Today, most Australians are related to settlers from Europe who first arrived about 200 years ago. English is the main language.

A SURFING COMPETITION IN SYDNEY, AUSTRALIA

Australian cattle ranches are called stations. There are many across the country.

THE ANIMALS

Kangaroo crossing!

GREEN SEA TURTLE

Many unusual animals live in Australia. Koalas, kangaroos, and wallabies raise their babies in pouches in their bellies. The duck-billed platypus is a mammal like us. But its babies hatch out of eggs!

KOALA

PLATYPUS

Green sea turtles are found off the coast and sometimes come up on land to get some sun.

WALLABIES

CROWN-OF-THORNS SEA STAR

In the coral reefs of the Great Barrier Reef, crown-of-thorns sea stars have become a problem. They hurt the underwater environment by eating corals.

THE SIGHTS

Fun in the water and on land

SURFER AT SNAPPER ROCKS, GOLD COAST

The Great Barrier Reef is Earth's largest living structure. It's off Australia's northeastern coast. Australia's beautiful beaches are popular surfing spots. There's even a city named Surfers Paradise!

SYDNEY OPERA HOUSE

Would you rather learn how to surf or scuba dive?

THE GREAT BARRIER REEF

The Sydney Opera House is one of Australia's most famous places to visit. It hosts plays, dances, and concerts.

LET'S GO!

Leap like a kangaroo

Red kangaroos can cover 25 feet (7.6 m) in a single leap. How does your longest leap compare to a jumping roo's?

You'll need:

- masking tape
- tape measure
- flat ground
- marker

1 Make a line on the ground with masking tape. This is the starting point of your jump.

2 Get a running start and jump from the line you just made. Remember to practice your jumping safely.

AUSTRALIA

3

Mark your landing spot with a piece of tape. Use the tape measure to measure the distance between the starting line and your landing spot.

4

Make several jumps and mark each jump with a piece of tape.

5

Label each try, "Jump 1," "Jump 2," "Jump 3," and so on.

6

Which jump was the longest? How does it measure up to a red kangaroo's?

CHAPTER 7

ANTARCTICA

GENTOO PENGUINS ON AN ICE
IN THE ANTARCTIC PENINSULA

THE LAND

A frozen landscape

Antarctica is Earth's coldest, driest, and windiest place. This landmass covers the South Pole.

There are no countries. But scientists from all over the world have set up research stations here to study the land, weather, and animals.

FACTS

SIZE
5,100,000 square miles (13,209,000 sq km)

HIGHEST MOUNTAIN
Vinson Massif

LOWEST PLACE
Byrd Glacier

Antarctica is the world's largest cold desert.

ANTARCTICA

AFRICA
ATLANTIC OCEAN
SOUTH AMERICA
INDIAN OCEAN
ANTARCTICA
PACIFIC OCEAN
AUSTRALIA
INDIAN OCEAN
QUEEN MAUD LAND
ENDERBY LAND
Weddell Sea
PENINSULA
RONNE ICE SHELF
Berkner Island
TRANSANTARCTIC MOUNTAINS
ANTARCTICA
ELLSWORTH LAND
Sea
Vinson Massif
16,067 ft (4,897 m)
Highest elevation in Antarctica
South Pole
EAST ANTARCTICA
WEST ANTARCTICA
SHACKLETON ICE SHELF
MARIE BYRD LAND
Amundsen Sea
Byrd Glacier
-9,416 ft (-2,870 m)
Lowest elevation in Antarctica
ROSS ICE SHELF
WILKES LAND
Roosevelt Island
Ross Island
Mount Erebus
Ross Sea
INDIAN OCEAN
Map Key
Mountain
Ice cap
Glacier
Ice shelf
Research station
0
600 miles
0
900 kilometers

What's your favorite season?

OLYMPUS RANGE IN VICTORIA LAND, ANTARCTICA

The Olympus mountain range surrounds Antarctica's Dry Valleys.

These valleys get their name from the high winds that constantly blast away snow, leaving the land bare.

THE WEATHER

Pack your coat!

It's no surprise—it is cold in Antarctica year-round. Temperatures rarely rise above freezing. The continent gets very little rain or snow. That makes Antarctica a big cold desert.

The thick layer of ice covering the continent actually took millions of years to build up.

A BLIZZARD NEAR THE SOUTH POLE

Sea birds such as penguins (above) and cormorants (left) feast on the plentiful fish that live in the waters around Antarctica.

THE ANIMALS

It's a penguin parade.

LEOPARD SEAL

It might seem like nothing could survive in Antarctica. But that's not the case. Some animals are built for life here. Emperor penguins live on Antarctica year-round.

HUMPBACK WHALE

Leopard seals hunt among the floating ice.

Blue and humpback whales swim through Antarctic waters in the summer.

EXPLORER SPOTLIGHT

Roald Amundsen was the first explorer to reach the South Pole.

He planted Norway's flag at the South Pole on December 14, 1911. He and his team risked their lives to explore the frozen continent.

They had to drag supplies across 900 miles (1,500 km) of ice and back again. They wore heavy furs. For 99 days, they lived off food such as dried meat, raisins, and cocoa (what chocolate is made of).

Amundsen's success helped people learn more about polar exploration and the conditions in Antarctica.

LET'S GO!

Take care of a penguin "egg"

Mommy and daddy emperor penguins take turns caring for their egg. The penguin parent holds the egg on its feet to keep it warm. Try taking care of your own egg.

You'll need:

one orange

1

Place the orange on your feet. Gently support it by squeezing it with your feet. This is your penguin egg.

2

Now try to walk around like a penguin. Remember to waddle with your feet together, supporting your egg.

EMPEROR PENGUIN PARENTS TAKING TURNS CARING FOR THEIR EGG

PARENT TIPS

YOU CAN REINFORCE AN UNDERSTANDING OF PLACE, DIRECTION, AND MAP READING BEYOND THE PAGES OF THIS BOOK.
The time you spend extending these concepts can pay off greatly. Geography can be an abstract concept for children. Often, our kids are magically transported from here to there—usually via the Parent Taxi Service! Involve your child in the planning of routes. Explain directionality using natural markers such as the rising and setting sun and the North Star. City kids can help determine which subway or bus lines to take using your transit system's map.

Here are some other activities you can do after reading National Geographic's *Little Kids First Big Book of the World.*

THREADS OF THE WORLD

(Search Strategy)
Many of the goods that we buy are actually produced and shipped from faraway places. Your child can build a solid understanding of this by rummaging through her closet. With your child, look at the tags on her clothes and note the country where each piece was made. Make a list and mark the locations on the world map in this book. Discuss any trends you notice with your child. Did more clothes come from any particular continent?

GEO JAMS

(Music)
Explore the origins of the music you listen to in your home. What kinds of instruments are used to make your child's favorite tunes? Where do they come from? Drums and shakers are great examples of instruments that are made differently depending on a people's culture and location. For example, Inuit musicians make drums out of wood and caribou skin. During dances, Cherokee women wear leg rattles made of tortoise shells with pebbles inside. Ask your child to draw a picture of an instrument he would create if designing one from scratch. See if you can make the instrument using regular household objects.

BLOCK PARTY

(Math)
Help your child use blocks to make a 3-D map of your neighborhood. Label the block that represents your house, the one that represents your child's school, the neighborhood playground, and so on. Younger children can trace blocks onto paper to make a 2-D map. Then, take the map with you on your next outing. Use it to navigate to your destination. Make a wrong turn? That's a great opportunity to teach your child about the importance of revising your work after you've tested it.

MAPS EVERYWHERE

(Arts and Crafts)

Displaying maps in your home is a great way to incorporate them into your routines. Maps can appear in unexpected places. (Check out shower curtain maps, map placemats, map posters, and map bulletin boards.) Hang a country or world map and insert push pins into all the places your family has visited. Or, have your child interview family members to find out where your family and their ancestors are originally from. Mark these locations on a map and include family pictures, if available. You can even create your own map puzzle. Give your child a map that you don't use and allow her to cut it into jigsaw-shaped pieces.

MAKE A MODEL

(Geography/Landforms)

Use modeling clay to form geographic features, such as islands, mountains, and valleys. If available, make models in a disposable baking dish with plasticine, a type of clay that doesn't absorb water. Pour water into the dish to model the water and land features. For younger kids, make expanding oceans. Draw the seven continents on a coffee filter. Roughly fill in the oceans in blue. Spray water on the filter and watch the blue "water" spread.

GAMES OF THE GLOBE

(Exercise)

Many popular sports originated in other places. With your child, research the roots of his favorite sport. Have the rules and equipment changed since the sport became popular here? If they have, try to organize a pick-up game of the sport that incorporates some of the original rules. For example, if your children's favorite sport is baseball, take a look at how cricket, the sport that inspired baseball, was played. How could you tweak your game to include some of the rules of cricket?

IMAGINARY ISLAND

(Creative Thinking)

Teach your child about map symbols and legends by having her create a map of an imaginary secret island. The island can be the location of anything: a pirate hideout, an alien spaceship landing site, a tropical resort for unicorns—you name it! The map must include symbols and a legend, or key, that explains what each symbol means.

VISIT ONLINE

(Technology)

For more geography education resources and map exploration tools, visit:

education.nationalgeographic.com/education

kids.nationalgeographic.com

nationalgeographic.com/kids-world-atlas/maps.html

GLOSSARY

ATLAS
a book of maps

CARAVAN
a group of people, usually traders, traveling across a desert in Africa or Asia

CLIMATE
the average weather conditions of a place

CONTINENT
one of the world's main expanses of land

DESERT
a dry area of land that receives fewer than ten inches (25 cm) of rain or snow a year

EQUATOR
an imaginary line around the Earth that divides the planet into northern and southern hemispheres, or halves

ERUPTION
the release of lava and/or gas from a vent in a volcano

EXPLORATION
the act of traveling through an unfamiliar area to learn about it

GLACIER
a slowly moving mass of ice usually found high up in mountains or near the poles

GLADIATORS
men trained to fight with weapons against other men or animals for sport

GONDOLA
a flat-bottomed boat that is commonly used as transportation through canals in Venice, Italy

GOODS
items such as food or clothing that are commonly sold in a marketplace

LANDMASS
a large chunk of land, such as a continent or a large island

MAMMAL
a warm-blooded animal whose young feed on milk produced by the mother

MOSAIC
a picture or pattern usually made by arranging pieces of glass or tile

MOSQUE
a place of worship for people of the Muslim religion

MYTHOLOGY
a collection of stories that belong to one culture or religion

OBSERVE
to notice something and believe it's important or figure out that it's not important

PILGRIMAGE
a religious journey usually made to a sacred place

PLATEAU
an area of high ground that is flat

PREY
animals that are hunted and killed by another animal for food

PYRAMID
a large structure with a square or triangular base and sloping sides that meet in a point at the top

RAIN FOREST
a dense forest that receives more than 60 inches (152 cm) of rain a year

SETTLER
a person who moves into an undeveloped area to live there

SPECIES
a group of similar organisms that can produce young

TERRITORY
an area of land under the control of another country's government

VOLCANO
An opening in Earth's crust (usually at the top of a mountain or hill) where lava, ash, and gases from deep inside Earth escape

INDEX

Boldface indicates illustrations.

A

Aboriginals 102, **102**
Africa
  animals **76-77, 80, 83, 86-87,** 87, 88, **88, 90-91**
  deserts 80, 83, **83**
  land and weather 80, 83
  maps 78-79, 80-81
  people 78, **78,** 84, **84-85**
  rain forests **82,** 83
  savannas 80
Alberta, Canada: bison **10-11**
Alpine marmots 53, **53**
Amazon rain forest, South America 30, 33, **33**
Amazon River, South America 30, **30**
Amundsen, Roald 118-119, **118-119**
Andes (mountains), South America 30, 36
Angkor Wat, Cambodia 72, **72-73**
Antarctica
  animals **110-111, 116-117,** 117, 120, **120-121**
  land and weather 112, 115
  map 112-113
  polar exploration 118-119, **118-119**
  research stations 112, **112**
Arches National Park, Utah **14**
Arcos de la Frontera, Spain **49**
Armadillos **36,** 37
Asia
  animals **70-71,** 71
  land and weather 64, 67
  maps 62-63, 64-65
  people **66,** 68, **68-69**
  rice growing 67, **67**
  temples **2-3,** 72, **72-73**
  traditions 68, 69
Atacama Desert, Chile 30, **30**
Australia
  animals **94-95, 96,** 104-105, **104-105,** 108, **108**
  coral reefs 105, 106, **106-107**
  land and weather 98, 101
  maps 96-97, 98-99
  outback 98
  people 102, **102-103**
Ayers Rock (Uluru), Australia 98, **98**

B

Basketball 18, **18**
Bayon Temple, Cambodia **2-3**
Bison **10-11**
Black Forest, Germany **48**
Blue Mosque, Turkey 74, **74-75**
Blue-winged kookaburra **96**
Brazil 29
  jaguar **26-27**
  rain forest **33**
  see also Rio de Janeiro
Burj Khalifa, Dubai, United Arab Emirates 73, **73**

C

Cairo, Egypt 78, **78**
Camels 36, **83**
Canada 13
  elk **12**
  see also Alberta; Nunavut
Caribou 53, **53**
Carnival 38, **38**
Castles 55, **55**
Chichén Itzá, Mexico **22**
Chimpanzees 90-91, **90-91**
China 62
  pandas 70, **70**
  see also Great Wall of China; Shanghai
Colosseum, Rome, Italy 54, **54**
Cormorants 116, **116**
Crete (island), Greece **48**
Crown-of-thorns sea stars 105, **105**

D

Deserts
  Africa 80, 83, **83**
  Antarctica 112, 115
  Asia 64, **66**
  Australia **100**
  North America 14
  South America 27, 30, **30**
Dry Valleys, Antarctica 114
Duck-billed platypus 104, **104**

E

Ecuador: white-water rafters **34-35**
Egypt
  pyramids 88, **88**
  see also Cairo
Elephants **2-3, 76-77,** 87
Elk **12**
Emperor penguins **116-117,** 117, 120, **120-121**
England. see London; Stonehenge
Etna, Mount, Sicily, Italy 56, **56-57**
Europe
  animals **49, 50, 52-53,** 53
  history 46, 50, 54-55
  land and weather 46, 49
  major rivers 46
  maps 44-45, 46-47
  people 50, **50-51,** 54
Everest, Mount, China-Nepal **64,** 65

F

Foxes 52, 53

G

Gentoo penguins **110-111**
Giraffes **86,** 87
Glaciers National Park, Argentina 32, **32**
Gobi desert, Asia **66**
Goodall, Jane 90-91, **90-91,** 92
Gorillas 87, **87**
Grand Canyon, Ariz. 22, **22**
Great Barrier Reef, Australia 105, 106, **106-107**
Great Wall of China, China 72, **72**
Green sea turtles 104, **104**
Greenland 12, **14**
Guanacos 36, **36**

H

Himalaya, Asia 64
Hippopotamuses **86,** 87
Humpback whales 117, **117**

I

Iceland: girl with lamb **50**
Inca 38, 39
India **68,** 71; *see also* Taj Mahal
Italy 54; *see also* Colosseum; Etna, Mount; Venice

J

Jaguar **26-27**

K

Kangaroos 104, 108, **108**
Kenya
  elephants **76-77**
  see also Masai Mara; Nairobi
Kilimanjaro, Mount, Tanzania 80, **82-83**
Koalas 104, **104**
Komodo dragons 71, **71**

L

Leopard seals 117, **117**
Lions 87, **87**
London, England **42-43**
Los Flamencos National Reserve, Chile **30**

M

Macaws **20-21,** 36, **36,** 37
Machu Picchu, Peru 38, **38-39**
Malaysia: tea plantation **66**
Manatees 20, **20,** 21
Masai Mara, Kenya: Masai children **84-85**
Maya 22
Mecca, Saudi Arabia **68-69,** 69
Mexico 12
  beach **16-17**
  pyramids 22, **22**
Michelangelo 58
Millaa Millaa Falls, Queensland, Australia **100-101**
Mongolia: desert **66**
Mont Saint-Michel, France **1**
Mosaics 74-75, **74-75**
Musk oxen 21, **21**

N

Nairobi, Kenya **84**
Neuschwanstein Castle, Germany **55**
North America
  animals **10-11, 12, 20-21,** 21
  cultures 18
  land and weather 14, 17
  languages 24
  maps 13, 15
  natural wonders 22
  people 18, **18-19**
North Pole 14
Nunavut, Canada: tobogganing **18-19**

O

Olympus Range, Antarctica 114, **114-115**
Owls 52, **52,** 53

P

Pandas 70, **70**
Penguins **110-111, 116-117,** 117, 120, **120-121**
Peru: stone ruins 38, **38-39**
Peruvian girl **34**
Peter, Carsten 56-57, **56-57**
Pink river dolphins 37, **37**
Poison dart frogs 37, **37**
Polar bears **20-21,** 21

Pyramids 22, **22,** 88, **88,** 125

R
Rain forests
  Africa **82,** 83
  Asia 64
  Central America 21
  South America 27, 33, **33,** 37
  Tasmania 98
Reindeer 53, **53**
Ring-tailed dragon lizard **94–95**
Rio de Janeiro, Brazil **28,** 38
Russia 44; see *also* St. Basil's Cathedral

S
Saguaro cactus **14**
Sahara, Africa 83, **83**
Shanghai, China 62, **62**
Shark Bay, Australia **94–95**
Sheep **49, 50**
Sistine Chapel, Vatican City 58
Soccer **34–35,** 35
South America
  animals **26–27, 36–37,** 37
  desert 27, 30, **30**
  land and weather 30, 33
  maps 29, 31
  people 34, **34–35,** 38, **38**
  rain forest 27, 33, **33,** 37
South Pole 112, 115, 118, **118**
Squirrel monkey **21**
Squirrels **52,** 53
St. Basil's Cathedral, Moscow, Russia **44**
Statue of Liberty, New York, N.Y. **22–23,** 23, 73
Stonehenge, England 54, **54–55**
Swaziland: students **84**
Switzerland: students **50**
Sydney, Australia: surfing **102–103**
Sydney Harbor, Sydney, Australia: storm **101**
Sydney Opera House, Sydney, Australia **106,** 107

T
Taj Mahal, Agra, India **60–61,** 74
Tanzania
  mountain **82–83**
  zebras **80**
Tasmania 98
Thailand: students **68**
Tigers **70–71,** 71
Tokyo, Japan 62, **63**
Tornadoes 16, **16**
Tulum, Mexico **16–17**
Tumucumaque National Park, Brazil **33**
Turkey 62; see *also* Blue Mosque

U
Uganda: rain forest **82**
Uluru (Ayers Rock), Australia 98, **98**
United States 12, 23
  tornadoes 16, **16**
  see *also* Arches National Park; Grand Canyon; Statue of Liberty
Ural Mountains, Europe-Asia 47

V
Venice, Italy: gondolas **50–51**
Vespucci, Amerigo 13
Victoria Falls, Zambia-Zimbabwe **88–89,** 89
Vietnam: bike riders **66**
Volcanoes 30, 56–57, **56–57,** 80, 125

W
Wallabies 104, **104–105**
World: maps 8, 9

Y
Yaks 71, **71**

Z
Zebras **80,** 88, **88**

PHOTO CREDITS

ABBREVIATIONS: AL: Alamy; GI: Getty Images; IS: iStockphoto; NGC: National Geographic Creative; SS: Shutterstock

Cover (St Basil's), Vladitto/SS; (Earth), leonello calvetti/SS; (tiger), Benjamin Jessop/IS; (fruit), Lori Epstein/NGC; (Sphinx & pyramid), Ian Stewart/SS; (Asian elephant), Lori Epstein/NGC; (cherry blossoms), Lori Epstein/NGC; (red-eyed tree frog), Mark Kostich/IS; (Statue of Liberty), james cheadle/AL; (Earth), leonello calvetti/SS; (hippo), Roy Toft/NGC; 1, Boris Stroujko/SS; 2–3, Jim Richardson/NGC; 4 (UP), BogdanBoev/SS; 4 (LO), Armando Frazao/SS; 5 (UP), Dave Pusey/SS; 5 (LO), frans lemmens/AL; 10–11, Peter Adams/Photographer's Choice/GI; 12, John E Marriott/All Canada Photos/GI; 14 (UP), PavelSvoboda/SS; 14 (LOLE), Colin D. Young/SS; 14 (LORT), Jo Ann Snover/SS; 16 (INSET), Todd Shoemake/SS; 16, BlueOrange Studio/SS; 17, Lane V. Erickson/SS; 18 (LE), blickwinkel/AL; 18 (RT), Aspen Photo/SS; 19, Design Pics Inc./AL; 20, Tom linster/SS; 20 (LOLE), Greg Amptman/SS; 20 (LORT), Jak Wonderly; 21 (LE), Dennis Jacobsen/SS;21 (RT), Mikhail Blajenov/SS; 22 (LE), Martin M303/SS; 22 (RT), Patryk Kosmider/SS; 23, Mike Tauber/Blend Images RM/GI; 24–25 (kids), Christopher Futcher/iStockphoto; 24–25 (UP), barbaliss/SS; 25 (music notes), argus/Shutterstock; 26–27, Mint Images/Art Wolfe/GI; 28, Catarina Belova/SS; 31 (UP), Steven Vidler/Eurasia Press/Corbis; 31 (LO), Nataliya Hora/SS; 32, elnavegante/SS; 33, Aaron Chervenak/AL; 34 (LE), Bartosz Hadyniak/Vetta/GI; 34 (RT), Ammit Jack/SS; 35, Digital Media Pro/SS; 36 (UP), David Thyberg/SS; 36 (LOLE), WitthayaP/SS; 36 (LORT), Marcos Amend/SS; 37 (LE), guentermanaus/SS; 37 (RT), Dirk Ercken/SS; 38, T photography/SS; 39, Lori Epstein/NGC; 40 (All), Lori Epstein/www.loriepstein.com; 41 (All), Lori Epstein/www.loriepstein.com; 42–43, Pawel Libera/Stone SubGI; 44, Tatiana Popova/SS; 48, Tom Plesnik/SS; 48 (INSET), Patrick Poendl/SS; 49, Lori Epstein/NGC; 50 (LE), Arctic Images/AL; 50 (RT), BSIP SA/AL; 51, Matthias Scholz/AL; 52 (INSET), seawhisper/SS; 52, blickwinkel/AL; 53 (LE), Andreas Gradin/SS; 53 (RT), Erick Margarita Images/SS; 54, JeniFoto/SS; 55 (UP), Cedric Weber/SS; 55 (LO), Belushi/SS; 56, Carsten Peter/NGC; 57 (UP), Carsten Peter/NGC; 57 (LO), Carsten Peter/NGC; 58, Lori Epstein/www.loriepstein.com; 59 (All), Lori Epstein/www.loriepstein.com; 60–61, Lori Epstein/NGC; 62 (LE), Oktay Ortakcioglu/Vetta/GI; 62 (RT), Sean Pavone/SS; 64, AntonSokolov/SS; 66 (inset UP), Thomas Bradford/IS; 66, David Edwards/NGC; 66 (INSET lo), Iakov Kalinin/SS; 67, Tom Wang/SS; 68 (UP), Hector Conesa/SS; 68 (LO), Lori Epstein/NGC; 69, Zurijeta/SS; 70, neelsky/SS; 70 (INSET), Hung Chung Chih/SS; 71 (LE), seastudio/IS; 71 (RT), Anna Kucherova/SS; 72, feiyuezhangjie/SS; 73 (LE), Luciano Mortula/IS; 73 (RT), Sophie James/SS; 74 (INSET), Oleg Golovnev/SS; 74–75, Matej Kastelic/SS; 75 (all INSETs), Lori Epstein/www.loriepstein.com; 76–77, Martin Harvey/Photolibrary RM/GI; 78, Lori Epstein/NGC; 80, fStop Images/Sean Russell/Brand X/GI; 82 (INSET), Boleslaw Kubica/SS; 82, Graeme Shannon/SS; 83, cdrin/SS; 84 (LE), Aleksandar Todorovic/SS; 84 (RT), Pal Teravagimov/SS; 85, boezie/IS; 86 (INSET), Roy Toft/NGC; 86, moizhusein/SS; 87 (LE), PRILL/SS; 87 (RT), Dave Pusey/SS; 88 (LE), Gerry Ellis/Digital Vision; 88 (RT), lexan/SS; 89, Przemyslaw Skibinski/SS; 90, Hugo Van Lawick/NGC; 91 (UP), Michael Nichols/NGC; 91 (LO), Michael Nichols/NGC; 92, Lori Epstein/www.loriepstein.com; 93 (All), Lori Epstein/www.loriepstein.com; 94–95, Paul Morton/E+/GI; 96, imageBROKER/AL; 98, Simon Bradfield/IS;100, Wouter Tolenaars/SS; 100 (INSET), ck10_9/IS; 101, CristinaMuraca/SS; 102, Penny Tweedie/GI; 103, frans lemmens/AL; 103 (INSET), LOOK Die Bildagentur der Fotografen GmbH/AL;104 (UP), Stephen Frink/Digital Vision; 104 (CTR), Martin Valigursky/SS; 104 (LO), John Carnemolla/IS; 105 (UP), Richard I'Anson/Lonely Planet Images/GI; 105 (LO), WaterFrame/AL; 106 (LE), GTS Production/SS; 106 (RT), Selfiy/SS 107, David Doubilet/NGC;108 (LE), Dirk Freder/IS; 108 (RT), Lori Epstein/www.loriepstein.com; 109 (All), Lori Epstein/www.loriepstein.com; 110–111, Wayne Lynch/All Canada Photos/GI; 112, Gordon Wiltsie/NGC; 114, Maria Stenzel/NGC; 115, Gordon Wiltsie/NGC; 116, Maria Stenzel/NGC; 116 (INSET), Dmytro Pylypenko/SS; 117 (LE), Keenpress/NGC; 117 (RT), Paul Nicklen/NGC; 118, Public Domain; 119 (LE), NOAA; 119 (CTR), Public Domain; 119 (RT), Public Domain; 120 (All), Lori Epstein/www.loriepstein.com; 121, Graham Robertson/Minden Pictures; 124, Pal Teravagimov/SS; 125, Tom linster/SS; 127, majeczka/SS

Published by National Geographic Partners, LLC.

Copyright © 2015 National Geographic Society. All rights reserved. Reproduction of the whole or any part of the contents without written permission from the publisher is prohibited.

NATIONAL GEOGRAPHIC and Yellow Border Design are trademarks of the National Geographic Society, used under license.

Staff for This Book
Priyanka Sherman, Amy Briggs, *Project Editors*

Eva Absher-Schantz, *Art Director*

Lori Epstein, *Senior Photo Editor*

Carl Mehler, *Director of Maps*

Juan José Valdés, *The Geographer*

Martha Sharma, *Geography Consultant*

Paige Towler, *Editorial Assistant*

Maureen J. Flynn, Julie A. Ibinson, Michael Fry, *Map Editors*

Michael McNey and Martin S. Walz, *Map Production*

Erica Holsclaw, *Special Projects Assistant*

Rachel Kenny, *Design Production Assistant*

Michael Cassady, *Rights Clearance Specialist*

Grace Hill, *Managing Editor*

Joan Gossett, *Senior Production Editor*

Lewis R. Bassford, *Production Manager*

George Bounelis, *Manager, Production Services*

Susan Borke, *Legal and Business Affairs*

Senior Management Team, Kids Publishing and Media
Nancy Laties Feresten, *Senior Vice President*
Jennifer Emmett, *Vice President, Editorial Director, Kids Books*
Julie Vosburgh Agnone, *Vice President, Editorial Operations*
Rachel Buchholz, *Editor and Vice President,* NG Kids *magazine*
Michelle Sullivan, *Vice President, Kids Digital*
Eva Absher-Schantz, *Design Director*
Jay Sumner, *Photo Director*
Hannah August, *Marketing Director*
R. Gary Colbert, *Production Director*

Digital
Anne McCormack, *Director*
Laura Goertzel, Sara Zeglin, *Producers*
Jed Winer, *Special Projects Assistant*
Emma Rigney, *Creative Producer*
Brian Ford, *Video Producer*
Bianca Bowman, *Assistant Producer*
Natalie Jones, *Senior Product Manager*

Since 1888, the National Geographic Society has funded more than 14,000 research, conservation, education, and storytelling projects around the world. National Geographic Partners distributes a portion of the funds it receives from your purchase to National Geographic Society to support programs including the conservation of animals and their habitats. To learn more, visit natgeo.com/info.

For more information, please visit nationalgeographic.com, call 1-877-873-6846, or write to the following address:

National Geographic Partners, LLC
1145 17th Street N.W.
Washington, DC 20036-4688 U.S.A.

For librarians and teachers: nationalgeographic.com/books/librarians-and-educators

More for kids from National Geographic: natgeokids.com

National Geographic Kids magazine inspires children to explore their world with fun yet educational articles on animals, science, nature, and more. Using fresh storytelling and amazing photography, *Nat Geo Kids* shows kids ages 6 to 14 the fascinating truth about the world—and why they should care. **kids.nationalgeographic.com/subscribe**

For rights or permissions inquiries, please contact National Geographic Books Subsidiary Rights: bookrights@natgeo.com

Hardcover ISBN: 978-1-4263-2050-7
Reinforced Library Edition ISBN: 978-1-4263-2051-4

Printed in Malaysia
21/IVM/11 (hardcover)
21/IVM/2 (RLB)